FINDING MY BELLA VITA

FINDING MY BELLA VITA

A story of family, food, fame and
working out who you are

PIA MIRANDA

hachette
AUSTRALIA

hachette
AUSTRALIA

Published in Australia and New Zealand in 2023
by Hachette Australia
(an imprint of Hachette Australia Pty Limited)
Gadigal Country, Level 17, 207 Kent Street, Sydney, NSW 2000
www.hachette.com.au

Hachette Australia acknowledges and pays our respects to the past, present and
future Traditional Owners and Custodians of Country throughout Australia
and recognises the continuation of cultural, spiritual and educational practices
of Aboriginal and Torres Strait Islander peoples. Our head office is located on
the lands of the Gadigal people of the Eora Nation.

A catalogue record for this
book is available from the
National Library of Australia

NATIONAL
LIBRARY
OF AUSTRALIA

ISBN: 978 0 7336 4983 7 (paperback)

Cover and picture section design by Christabella Designs
Front cover photographs courtesy of Tina Smigielski Photography and Shutterstock
Back cover *Survivor* photograph courtesy of Endemol Shine Australia/Nigel Wright – Wrightphoto;
other back cover photographs from the author's collection
All picture section photographs from the author's collection
Typeset in 12.5/20 pt Scala Pro by Bookhouse, Sydney
Printed and bound in Australia by McPherson's Printing Group

For Lily and James

PROLOGUE

Every day on top of the dirt is a good day.

NONNA ANGELINA

There were many times while writing this book that I wondered . . . *Oh my God, am I unhinged? Am I annoying? Could I possibly be the arsehole that @Aus_mum85 told me I was on Instagram?* But writing about my life has also enabled me to see how far I have come, how much I have changed and how all of my imperfections are actually okay. It is a strange thing, to live and breathe and walk through the world never quite sure of who you are, but it's a sensation that many of us are familiar with. If you are one of the lucky ones, this is only your lot when you are young – as you age and settle into yourself, you find the things that matter to you, that soothe your soul and bring you joy. For some of us, the searching never ends.

They say age brings acceptance and wisdom, but I have oscillated throughout my life, even as I've grown older, between this state and the anxiety of being buffeted by what society said defined beauty or belonging, by wanting but not knowing exactly what it was I wanted or how to get it, and by fearing life being snatched away. This fear is what motivated my obsessive drive to matter, to be loved and to not be forgotten. It took a long time for me to realise that the body I was born with should be celebrated, despite its betrayals and mysteries. And to genuinely know yourself is to know all the parts of you and all the fragments of life that create who you are. We are not defined by one single thing, but billions of things, big and small, that direct our thoughts and responses. None of it is set in stone. You can change things about yourself, but I now know that it is often the thing you dislike most about yourself that makes you special . . . so how much do we really need to change after all?

It is kinda funny that for many I am forever a teenage girl, captured in celluloid as Josie, a young woman not sure of where she belonged but determined to live her life honestly and powerfully after growing tired of being defined by others. I would go on to play many other roles in film, on TV and on stage; I would put myself out there on panels and TV shows and prove to myself and others I was the ultimate Survivor. It is only now, looking back at my life to this point, that I can appreciate where I am. In order to come to that understanding I had to pull apart the jigsaw and sit with all the moments and memories of the people who helped build the person I am – the grief, the fear, the joy, the doubt and disappointments, the loves and triumphs, hates and the hurt.

I hope that by sharing my story I will help other misfits find their place. I hope that it might show that the pressure of growing up between two cultures and having to navigate the constant push and pull of tradition can actually mean your world is richer. Most of all, I hope my story inspires everyone to know that you are never defined by what has been before. You can be whoever you strive to be and when people expect little from you, that is their weakness, not yours. I hope we can all find our own beautiful life. I think I have.

But to get to that point, we have to go back to a small volcanic island in the sea not far from Sicily. It is here that *Finding My Bella Vita* begins. Here it is . . .

PART ONE

CHAPTER ONE

Avoid the bad, love the good, because
things change in a moment.
SICILIAN PROVERB

Sure, this is a story about me, but we are all the people we've become because of the people who came before us. The women in my family played a huge part in helping shape me. Strong, defiant women who were born into a world that wasn't quite ready to see them as equals – a world we still have to navigate and battle against, but also one that has given those of us who followed amazing opportunities. So I want to begin by telling you about a woman who had to push against tradition and fear to make a life for herself and because she did that, I was born. As it turns out, I am not the hero of my story; my nonna, Angelina, is.

When I was a kid I would listen to Nonna's stories about her life growing up in a very different place. She was born in 1921 in the Mediterranean, on a volcanic island off the coast of Sicily; a place of coarse black sand, the smell of sulphur in the air, thermal springs and relentless burning sun. All she knew was her small and simple life. She felt ordinary and insignificant, cemented to the island, and she had no thoughts of ever leaving. Angelina passionately believed that God smiled on her every day. She was the youngest of ten and as the baby of the family she felt comforted, protected, loved.

Angelina grew into a sweet fifteen-year-old and her daily life consisted of helping with the farming and looking after the house with her mother. There was no education available for a girl like her, but she learnt to become proficient with her hands, sewing, cooking and looking after the goats. One day she was sunning herself while shelling peas for a party when an intense wave of contentment and love overtook her body and she wondered if it was a sign from God. She looked up to her mother and said, 'I think I'll stay here forever and look after this place and never leave your side. This is enough,' she said. 'I'm happy.'

What Angelina didn't know that day was that across the water in Palermo, a young orphan named Salvatore had heard about a man with ten daughters who was having a party to try to find some husbands for those that weren't yet married. Salvatore was small in stature and big in personality, and his athletic body and tanned skin had always been a moderate hit with the ladies, but the clock was ticking and he was feeling the pressure to find himself a suitable wife. Hearing of this party piqued his interest.

'Ten?' he thought. 'Surely the statistics are in my favour that one of them might be suitable for me?' (Okay, let's just admit he probably didn't use the word 'statistics', because he hadn't been taught to read or write, but it works for the story. Anyway, back to Sicily in 1936 . . .)

Salvatore jumped on a boat with a couple of his buddies and they headed off for a boys' weekend to Vulcano, one of the smaller Aeolian Islands north of Sicily. They each had hopes of finding themselves a lovely buxom woman to settle down and have children with. Big boobs were all the rage back then in Sicily.

When they turned up on the dock, the group of mates were shocked by the island's undeveloped landscape and dilapidated housing as well as the pungent smell of sulphur. They thought about aborting their mission, but they had committed to finding wives and had come a fair way, so off they went. When they finally found the home where the party was being held, the festivities had already begun; it was surprisingly fun and full of energy. Set outdoors under the stars, the balmy weather had everyone in a festive mood, helped by the amazing food and wine being served up. Sicily is known for its seafood and pasta dishes, and food was a big focus for any celebration; no party would have been complete without fish, pasta and biscotti, *sfinge* and grappa, even in the poorer rural areas like Vulcano. The boys danced and mingled and had such a good time that some of them forgot they were on the lookout for a bride. Not Salvatore though; in true Sicilian style he was like a dog with a bone – he didn't want to leave until he had struck gold.

Parties were a rare treat on the island and as Angelina looked around the room she was filled with a sense of excitement and adventure. She had her dark hair pulled up into a loose bun and was wearing a new blue dress that hugged her more than ample bosom. She felt the loveliest she had ever felt in her modest fifteen years. She may have been the baby of the family, but on this night she was a young woman charged with an energy she hadn't felt before.

It was early in the evening when she looked up and saw a darkly tanned boy staring at her intensely. He wasn't tall, but he looked fit and strong, and she couldn't help noticing his amazing blue eyes. He seemed to stand apart from everyone else and his serious look caught her attention. After a moment they shared a shy smile and he walked up to introduce himself. Then Salvatore asked her very sweetly if she would like to dance.

Angelina could tell that there was more to this boy than he was letting on. He had an air of bravado about him, but he was charming and attentive and they talked and danced into the early hours of the morning. As they danced close she felt an unfamiliar surge of desire. It was an over-whelming and delightful feeling and, combined with the rush of being the recipient of unbridled attention, it made her feel dizzy. This was the first time she felt like someone saw her, really saw into her soul, and it was as terrifying as it was breathtaking. Most girls her age were engaged or married and she had mostly given up on that idea for herself, but that night she felt a thrilling sense of possibility.

Angelina didn't want the party to end. But of course, no matter how much you want time to pause, it keeps ticking on. Eventually the music stopped and all the guests, including Salvatore, left.

◆

Angelina woke early the next morning and was cleaning the kitchen when she heard a cough behind her. She turned to see Salvatore standing at the door with a bunch of flowers and a cheeky smile, and it felt like her heart was going to stop beating. That was the start of a magical two-year courtship for the couple, and it was a courtship in every sense. For almost two years Angelina refused to give in to Salvatore's physical advances, and even though he tried to woo her he respected Angelina's commitment to her God-fearing chastity. When she turned seventeen he could wait no longer and they were finally married in the small white church that she had been worshipping in every

Sunday for her whole life. The church was ordinary and modest, with a row of cobbled stairs that led to the entrance. Angelina's dress was simple and meticulously sewn by her mother, and although it was made from basic cotton with a plain piece of tulle as a veil, the small embroidered sleeves and the starkness of the white fabric made her feel elegant and grown-up. The cream-coloured paint on the church's walls was peeling off in some places, but the enormous picture of Jesus and the Madonna hanging prominently above the altar made the whole space feel grand to her. As she walked up the aisle and looked into Salvatore's eyes, Angelina knew her new life was about to start and felt a combined sense of fear and belonging. When they were pronounced husband and wife, Salvatore leant in and kissed her forcefully and passionately on the lips with all of the pent-up energy of a young man in love. Years later she would tell her granddaughters (me included) that this was her first kiss, ever, as she encouraged us to rebuff advances from any boy we were dating and never let them touch us until we were married. Sure, Nonna.

What Nonna didn't realise, as she began her new life as a married woman, was that she, along with other women around the world, was about to send her husband off to war. Some would never return and others would return broken. Nonna learnt the harsh lesson that her fate and that of her new husband was determined not by something they did or desired, but by a wider world that was rapidly changing. Decisions made in government chambers thousands of miles away would irrevocably alter the future they were anticipating. That's the thing about war; the actions of just one person can destroy so many lives. So, in a cruel twist of fate, not long after marrying and only the day after Angelina discovered she was pregnant, Salvatore was shipped off to fight in the navy. And, unfortunately, this is where a new chapter of their love story begins.

CHAPTER TWO

Death finds everyone and the earth renews itself.
SICILIAN PROVERB

Soon after the wedding the newlyweds had moved to the larger island of Lipari and, although it was not much larger than Vulcano, Angelina found it unfamiliar and lonely without her husband. Her pregnancy was not easy and news of the horrors of war would reach her and make her cry. She tried to enjoy the feeling of a new life growing inside her, but a darkness followed her like an unwelcome passenger. Salvatore had promised he would return for the birth of their first child, but as the due date grew closer and still he wasn't home, sadness clouded her every thought and action. She was scared she would never see Salvatore again and worried constantly that something would go wrong with their child.

Southern Italians are very superstitious; they look for signs in all sorts of places and there is a belief that the gift of a divine sixth sense runs through their blood. Angelina's impending sense of doom was difficult to shake and when she went into labour she carried not the excitement she was expecting, but fear and dread. When it suddenly began, the labour was a shock to her young body and the women surrounding her bellowing instructions in a furious manner left her feeling very alone. This was definitely not the joyous experience she had prayed for. The pain went on and on, intensifying into a searing agony that felt as if her body was being torn apart. For a brief moment she thought she was going to die and she prayed to the Madonna to save her. Then, suddenly, there was no pain, just peace and silence. Angelina had witnessed enough births to know that silence was not good and she held her breath as she waited for her baby to cry.

She could hear commotion and panic from the women who had only moments before been yelling instructions to her and she shut her eyes. She didn't need to ask the question; she knew this day of joy had turned into one of despair and death.

When Salvatore finally made it home on leave to see his new family, he walked in with a beaming smile, but discovered an empty cot and a broken wife. Devastated, he stayed with Angelina for as long as he could, but the duty of war would eventually call him back and he returned to his ship. Before departing, he left Angelina a new gift – another life growing inside her, a boy who would bring her joy and mend her despair.

As the war raged, Salvatore's trips home would come sporadically. Sal would surprise Angelina with a visit and her world would feel complete for a few short weeks. Her anxiety for him was a constant though, as there were so many near misses. She was worried God would soon come for his soul like he had so many others.

Salvatore was a gunner on his ship and he was good at it; he had a masterful eye and a fierce, stubborn heart that made him one of the most liked and consistent men in his naval squadron. The fighting had been long and arduous, dragging on for years, but Salvatore's steely determination and patriotism kept pushing him forward. Like most of the poorer men in Sicily, Salvatore was uneducated and he had been taught from a young age to find value in hard work, not in deep thought. So although he didn't grasp the complexities of the war he was fighting or question the ethics of risking his life for fascist regimes, he was led by his passion and loyalty for the country he loved and the people he had left behind. Not everyone gets to be on the right side of history.

In 1943, Operation Husky, the Allied invasion of Sicily, was just taking hold and Italian naval ships were under incredible pressure as the large campaign to take down Mussolini and his fascist regime began. There was an elevated sense of stress among the naval officers as the casualties grew and the number of deaths became overwhelming. These things were always on Salvatore's mind, but he never stopped as he blindly fought for what he thought was right. In a strange twist of fate, a day finally came when he had to stop. He was preparing to take his place at his regular gunning spot when suddenly his stomach churned and he felt his insides catch fire as he doubled over in pain. His stomach cramps were excruciating and he began throwing up all over himself. As he lay on the wet tiles, vomiting, Sal saw his best mate standing above him.

'You look terrible,' his mate said.

'That bastard whitebait got me, I think,' Sal said and groaned. The moment he mentioned the fish he had eaten, he was vomiting again.

'I'll take your place tonight, *migliori*,' his friend said.

Even though Sal knew it was his mate's long overdue night off, he couldn't argue. He could barely stand. There was no way he could fire a gun. He felt a pat on his back and heard some reassuring words that he couldn't quite decipher, then he passed out.

◆

He wasn't sure how long he slept, but an epic boom woke Sal and he struggled to his feet. Gathering his thoughts he realised their ship had been hit. He raced up to the deck to check on his friend who had taken over his post. Instead he found a gaping hole where his cannon had been and was shocked to find only a bloody foot. It took him a second to realise what was in front of him and what it meant. Sal was pushed back by a crowd of men scrambling to safety. He was alive and his mate was dead. The reality of his tragic luck set in.

'Whitebait,' he thought. 'I was saved by some miniature fish left in the sun for too long. How is that God's plan?' He pondered on his dead baby and best friend and wondered if God was punishing him, and for the first time he questioned whether there was anyone watching over him at all. He could feel a dark volcanic anger bubbling away in his blood and he was scared of what would happen if it finally erupted.

◆

Angelina remained at home while this tragedy and the many others that war brought unfolded in her husband's life, raising their child as best she could on her own. With every visit home, she could see Sal's usually bright eyes becoming darker and his soul becoming harder to read. There was little contact from him during those years of war; sometimes it was six months between visits, sometimes a year, but every time he was home, she felt that God was on their side and maybe things would be all right, that he would be all right. It was getting hard to survive without him; wartime rationing meant food was scarce and with so many of its men fighting in the war, the island community was struggling, and so was Angelina. She took small jobs sewing and cleaning to make money, but there was barely enough to buy food for her and her son, Renato.

The early years of their child's life unfolded without his father in the house. Following one of Sal's rare visits, Angelina found she was pregnant again with a baby that thrived in her belly despite these difficult conditions. When he was born Angelina looked into his dark black eyes and knew this boy would find trouble; he had a stubbornly determined and mischievous spirit that was obvious even then. She named him Vincenzo, which means 'to conquer'.

As the boys grew, Vincenzo kept Angelina busy. He was a feisty firecracker who was always getting into trouble. The war finally ended and yet she received no word from Sal. She didn't know if he was alive or dead. Looking after Renato and Vincenzo helped distract her from dark thoughts, but the fear was ever present and only God was there to listen. Though Angelina didn't know it, Salvatore was alive and was so traumatised that he was too terrified to travel in a vehicle in case it was blown up. So he walked for thirty-six days before finally getting a boat and eventually making it home to his beloved family.

When she saw him, Angelina finally let out the tears she'd been holding in for so many years. Sal was home and they could start their life as a family. God had blessed them as she'd hoped He would. But, like most post-war family stories, the jubilance of survival and reuniting was quickly followed by the reality of the shattered world they had to live in. There was little food and no work – the ration for their family of four was only 200 grams of bread a day. As she prepared for the winter, Angelina wandered around town gathering up flags she found among the rubble to make clothes for her children. With his family often hungry, Salvatore wrestled with an overwhelming sense of failure that tortured his proud Sicilian heart. He obsessed over how to change their fate, which was looking more hopeless with every day that passed. There were rumblings around town about free tickets to Australia, where there were opportunities waiting for men who were willing to work hard. Salvatore started to wonder if he could go and then come back and *migliorare la vita* (improve their life).

Sal was a complex mix of a man; he had an inflated Sicilian ego with the soul of a scared child. He saw things in black and white. There was an anger that had always burned inside him and, as his circumstances grew more challenging, he worried that the fire of that anger would engulf him or, worse, incinerate everything and everyone around him. He was known for his passionate attitude, and although his fervour for an attractive woman was never fully dimmed by marriage, his love for his family overrode everything. Finally, like many young men with big hearts and no prospects, he decided to join a group looking for a better life for their families by heading to Australia. In doing that, they all left those families behind.

Nonna never shared much information about what those long weeks on the ship were like for her husband. I don't think she ever really knew. But I do know that many of the boats were overcrowded and the men lived in dormitory-style accommodation onboard. They passed the time playing cards and sharing stories about the families they had left behind, but Salvatore didn't talk much about any of it to Angelina. He kept the past locked away deep inside, a trick he had learnt when his parents had died of the Spanish flu while he was young and he was shipped off to a live with a family that cared little for him. With his determined spirit and a capacity to push down his feelings and just get on with things, Salvatore arrived in Australia ready to improve his life and that of his family.

Angelina was alone again, struggling to look after the boys and herself while waiting for news. I wonder if she ever looked back to that moment with her mother when she was fifteen, when she said that everything she wanted was right there and that she never wanted to leave. The war years had changed everything. Now it seemed to her the islands offered only hardship and early death. She felt the only help and protection she could hope for would come from Jesus and the Madonna, so she prayed. She prayed through her starvation, she prayed when her hungry children screamed, she prayed for work and she prayed for her family to be reunited.

It would be two years before her prayers were answered and Angelina and her sons finally boarded a boat to reunite with Salvatore in Australia after facing another trauma: a tearful and dramatic farewell to her siblings and parents as she left the islands that had been her home since birth. The moment the ship set sail, however, Angelina looked up and saw the sun shining through the clouds, and she knew God was with her. She wrapped her two boys up in her arms and they watched Lipari and Vulcano disappear into the distance.

◆

My father, Vincenzo, says he doesn't remember anything about this trip, it's just a black hole in his mind, so I sometimes wonder if he inherited his father's capacity for locking his feelings away. He was six years old at the time.

The journey to a new land would take nearly eight weeks and when Angelina finally stepped foot onto Australian soil, nothing was as she expected. Salvatore met her at the ship and the first home they shared was a small, dank rural house with a dirt floor. The house was surrounded by hundreds of pigs, who would scratch and bang on the door all night long. It was worse than anything she could ever have imagined. She sobbed quietly into her blankets at night, praying to God to help her return to Italy and the home she loved. She was homesick and wanted to leave every day, but Salvatore and the boys needed her to be strong, so she locked her pain away deep inside and pushed through one day at a time. (You may notice a theme emerging here. *Omerta*, the mafia code of honour that decreed silence was an obligation, has often seemed very pertinent to how my forebears sometimes chose to live.)

Eventually God did smile on Angelina and the family moved to a small town called Tatura, in rural Victoria. Here, her new home had a floor and windows and no paddock of pigs just outside the walls. The homesickness abated and she created a real home. In Tatura, Angelina and Salvatore were blessed with another baby boy they called Giorgio. Together, they farmed tomatoes, which were supplied to make White Crow tomato sauce, and they started to see their dreams come to life. The constant worry about finding food became a memory – Angelina had so many tomatoes to cook with, she could make fresh passata for their pasta every night.

But there were still worries. Vincenzo was getting into all sorts of trouble in this small town, often coming home beaten and bloody from fights at school. Nobody liked wogs in 1960s Australia; derogatory comments were common in the school playground and the homemade salami that he took for lunch just added fuel to the fire. Vincenzo, who had inherited his father's simmering anger, 'refused to take shit' (in his words) and fought back with his fists. Apart from those moments, it was a pretty good life, but after years of contented country life, Salvatore's restless spirit wanted more. They decided to try their luck in the big city.

The move to Melbourne was a good one for the family and city life suited them all. Angelina felt completely settled at last. Some of her sisters had come to Australia by this point and were close by, so the pang for Italy lessened. Salvatore opened a fruit shop and changed from being gruff and angry a great deal of the time to become a contented man with confidence and purpose. Angelina noticed how he strode around with his chest puffed out, a Camel cigarette balanced on his ear as he greeted his customers with a smile and a look of pride. Although the land of the volcanoes called to her from time to time, its voice was getting softer and mostly only came at night, when Angelina put her head on the pillow and tried to fall asleep to the loud sound of the trains rattling through Carnegie station.

The only hint of worry that my grandfather faced in those years related to Italian turf wars at Prahran Market, where he bought his produce. Sal was a man of strict principles; he wanted to run his business and look after his family with a proud heart and without answering to anyone.

'We are Australian now,' he would tell his boys, 'and we must leave all thoughts of the old country behind.' Sal's attitude was what had helped him survive those turbulent years, but perhaps it was also what led to his life being cut so short.

◆

On the last day of Salvatore's life, he grabbed his Australian driver's licence, of which he was so proud, popped his packet of Camel cigarettes into his back pocket and grabbed a few coins for a coffee. He kissed his beloved Angelina then headed out into the still-dark early morning to make his way to the markets before the boys were even stirring.

Later that day, two messengers of death came to Angelina's door and gave her the news: her husband had died in a freak accident at the market. Italians know how to express grief, and so her wailing began immediately. The police officers held her as she cried, but she fell to the ground.

When her wailing stopped, an officer handed her the contents of Salvatore's pockets: half a pack of Camels, a few coins and the Australian driver's licence. She slowly walked over to the table that was set for dinner with a beautiful red-and-white-checked tablecloth and matching serviettes. Angelina kissed the items, grabbed a serviette and wrapped up Sal's belongings. She tied the serviette in a knot and swore she'd never open it again.

Maybe it was just a terrible accident. I guess we will never know how my nonno ended up crushed between two truck trays, but I have always thought it sounded suspicious. In the 1960s there were a lot of strange 'accidents' at the markets, especially involving people who wouldn't fall into line. The explanations Nonna was given never quite made sense, but she wasn't thinking straight because grief was all she had time for. God was not smiling on them anymore. Salvatore was not coming home.

I have always imagined that as the truck reversed, my nonno must have looked up and taken a last panicked gasp because he knew his story was about to end. Then he was gone. Forever. I have always wondered what it must feel like to suddenly realise you are in the last paragraph of your story. My nonno had survived five years of war, but two trucks and one lousy second was all it took for him to be lost. I never got to meet him. I wish I did.

Though Nonna's grief never really subsided, at some point she gathered herself; she had three boys to raise on her own and they would need her strength and comfort. She would again have to draw on all her resilience to keep going.

So, as Salvatore's story ended, another chapter of Angelina's began. She was now a broken matriarch, but also a beacon of love for her boys. Her beloved and head-strong Vincenzo quit school in order to support the family, taking over the business and staying by Angelina's side as they faced a future together without Salvatore.

CHAPTER THREE

We learn by standing on the shoulders of the wise.

SICILIAN PROVERB

Nonna may have sworn that she would never open the package that held the contents of her husband's short life, but I had other ideas. When I was in kindergarten I found it hidden away and, from then on, I was obsessed with opening it in secret. I would cross my chubby legs on the carpet of her little Carnegie unit and search for that mysterious packet of goodies that I knew was stashed in the back of the Franco Cozzo sideboard. I would quietly untie the knot in the red-and-white serviette and pray to God that I wouldn't be caught, even though I knew God would be mad with me for doing it. I loved holding Nonno's driver's licence in my hands and I would stare at his picture, wondering whether he would have liked me. The face of my grandfather gave away no secrets, but I could sense a mix of fear and anger in the bright eyes that glared back at me, as though he knew what was coming for him. The smell of stale cigarettes and the feel of the old coins made me giddy with nostalgia for something I'd never known.

There was a connection to my nonno that even as a child I knew was an important part of who I was. I felt like I knew him, like I could feel him in my heart, even though I was also terrified of him and his foreboding stare. As I've grown older I've recognised that there is an essence of him that I carry with me, the spirit of a fighter, but also a shared darkness that I would continuously have to wrestle with. Whenever I have grappled with the bleak elements of my soul I always come back to his face and the darkness I could see in his eyes. Somehow even my childhood self knew this. So I would stare at Salvatore's face, knowing that we would always be connected not by experience, but by character.

Growing up in suburban Melbourne, I was lucky to have so much of both my parents' families around us. I don't know much about my parents' courtship other than the fact that they met at a squash court where Dad played and that they got engaged very quickly. There was talk that if my nonno was alive there would have been no way he would have let my dad marry someone who wasn't Italian, but my mum is pretty charming so I always believed she could have won him over. Dad was adamant that would never have been the case – I guess we will never know.

It's weird to think that if Nonno hadn't had that tragic accident I may not be here.

My sister, Nicole, was born in 1969 and I followed four years later. I came along on 15 June 1973, the year *The Exorcist* was a box office hit and Queen Elizabeth II opened the Sydney Opera House. Funnily enough, as I got older, both exorcism and drama would feature in my days. Mum's labour with me was quick and slippery. I flew out of her with only about twenty minutes warning, so she was lucky to make it into the foyer of Cabrini Hospital in Malvern. I still like to arrive early. Lateness stresses me out.

I always felt lucky to have an older sister, and Nicole and I were very close, even though I could be overexcitable and annoying. I talked a lot. My parents used to tease me, saying I had 'verbal diarrhoea'. When I was a toddler I would obsessively follow my sister around the house calling out 'Cole' repeatedly, and Nicole would yell to Mum, 'Make her stop!' She still loved me though. When I was very small she would unwittingly torture me by trying to shove me into a tiny toy pram and wheel me around like one of her dolls. My first memory is of Mum in stitches, trying to tell my sister to stop because I had grown too big for the pram yet not being able to help me because she was laughing too hard. I remember looking down at my legs and then up at my sister with her face showing fierce determination as she tried to squish me in, while I wished myself smaller to make her happy.

I started dancing when I was two. In keeping with wanting to do everything my sister did, I would scream and cry when she was in ballet class because I wanted to join in. I was lucky that my Aunt Rosslyn owned a wonderful ballet school and told my mum to just let me have a go. I leapt out of my mother's arms and my love affair with ballet began.

When I wasn't at home, at school or at ballet, I would split my time between my nonna's and my nanna's. I'm an Australian with Italian and Irish heritage. To some that might seem like two very different worlds, but as a kid it was just how my family was.

My nanna and grandfather on my mother's side were as strong an influence on my upbringing as my nonna. They too showered me with unconditional love and had a warm home filled with good food and happiness. My grandfather grew up in Malvern and was a St Kevins boy, while Nanna went to Convent of the Good Shepherd and lived in Middle Park, South Melbourne Football Club country. Funny that South Melbourne is known as the Bloods because love for that team subsequently ran through all of our veins. Nanna had a cool, fashion-forward bob and a timelessly chic look, and Grandfather had a sweet Bing Crosby/Fred Astaire kind of vibe. When they were young, the two of them spent their time hanging out on Middle Park Beach and going to dances and the movies.

By the time I got to know them, they were just cosy old Nanna and Grandfather. They never strayed far from where they grew up. They had a huge house on an old disused family dairy in Malvern, and I would spend afternoons hanging out in the abandoned car yard or skulking through the remnants of the old dairy looking for adventure. They loved where they lived and I did too. I adored being at their place, watching TV in front of the gas heater, eating biscuits and drinking tea. Cousins would pop in sporadically so it was often a house filled with people and noise. Grandfather worked at the ABC and he would bring home piles of light green paper that I would spend hours drawing on while Nanna served me snacks. It was childhood bliss.

After school was reserved for those happy times at Nanna's house while weekends were mostly for Nonna, and they were just as magical. Often, we would start by catching up on *Days of Our Lives* and *The Young and the Restless* (or in her accent *Days of a Dai* and *Young in the Wrestle*). She would watch the episodes earlier in the week and record them so we could rewatch them together, with me explaining any plot points she missed because of the language barrier. We would cook together, and take trips to the fruit shop via church to light a candle. I didn't mind going to church with Nonna because St Anthony's in Glen Huntly was huge and atmospheric, filled with lots of other Italian nonnas who warmed my heart with their mix of kindness and hysteria.

She called me 'Paparedda' and I loved it. 'Paparedda, Paparedda,' she would coo lovingly when I walked in the door or when she cuddled me on the green velvet couch. I didn't know at the time what it meant, but it made me happy, I think because I loved the way she said it in her thick Italian accent. My mum told me she thought it meant 'Little Duck', but my sister said she had heard it meant 'vagina that has wet itself', and as I did have a penchant for peeing my pants when I laughed too hard, I thought she might be right. Nonna would never tell me, she said it didn't matter, so I just went with it. Turns out 'duck' is the correct trans-lation, which I found slightly disappointing. I did walk like a duck from all of the ballet I was doing, so I guess it suited me.

When we were in primary school, the paintings of Jesus in the garden of olives in Nonna's spare bedroom used to really freak us out, so Nicole and I were never all-in on the idea of staying over unless we were together. But that was only a night-time worry, the days were always fun.

Our mornings would begin with Vegemite toast folded in half, dipped in a sugary cup of white tea (don't knock it until you've tried it). Then we'd prepare food with Nonna for the rest of the day, just in case visitors showed up. And they often did. I would sit in Nonna's kitchen, rolling gingerbread or stuffing artichokes under the watchful eye of a framed picture of Jesus whose heart would light up and glow red when he was plugged in. (Side note – I would 100 per cent have one of these in my house today if I could find one.) Nicole, Nonna and I would sit and talk about life and religion while Nonna's canary, whose name was Budgie, whistled and kept us company. Nonna's new husband was a life-sized teddy bear she sat in the hallway. Whenever we mentioned the idea of her marrying again, Nonna would reply, 'Why? I have him!' and point to the huge bear in a green top hat.

It was the late 1970s, and even at that young age I remember Nonna's food being so fresh and simple. Most of the ingredients were bought from the local grocer, where she would always swipe a plum or apricot, shoving it in my pocket and whispering, 'Shhh, for later.' I guess that's why I didn't feel bad about the lip gloss I shoplifted in Year 8.

◆

Those days and nights with Nonna gave me a love of food as well as an obsession with the afterlife. To say that Nonna, my sister and I were collectively obsessed with both would be an understatement.

Ceremony and tradition are an important part of Italian life and there was nothing more appealing to my Italian side of the family than events involving God, death and curses. Some of Nonna's sisters eventually moved to Australia and started their own families, and visits to their houses would usually entail curse removal. This sounds intense, but it was a pretty ordinary event for us. When the zias (aunts) got together, they enjoyed holding a bowl of water and oil above my head while they hummed and cried in an effort to remove my curses, which they described as exceptionally strong as I apparently had a natural tendency to attract them. (Funnily enough, there is a brief shot in *Looking for Alibrandi* where Josie's nonna does the same thing while Josie is studying in the kitchen – no acting was required there.) I didn't mind all of this palaver too much because I really hated being cursed and I was always given food as a reward when the curses were gone. I'll do anything for a free snack. I also truly believed them when they told me that this was all a part of my journey toward being a visionary, which was apparently my destiny. They gave me the impression that I was going to be the next child of Fátima – something I pondered for longer than I should have, given I showed no aptitude for precognition.

While I quite enjoyed these dramatic cleansing sessions, my sister found them relentlessly disturbing. Most terrifying to her was when they would stand us against a wall and pray loudly while staring at our auras until one of them would eventually cry out and fall to the floor. I would be thrilled if I made anyone collapse because I thought it meant that I was truly blessed and that they could see

God in me. I remember after one particularly long session standing by the wall, they cried out, 'She has a halo, it's blue!' and I was fucking thrilled. I had always suspected that I was a vessel for the Holy Spirit and this just proved it. Cake please.

Being told that I had a tendency to attract curses may sound scary, but I was much luckier than my sister, who was told she was susceptible to the odd possession. She was a little more sensitive to these accusations than I was, and thought that meant she was going to hell. During one particularly drawn-out session, Nicole cried hysterically from fear and dropped the bowl of holy water she had been holding. The bowl smashed on the floor, confirming to our zias that not only was she possessed, but that the devil himself made her do it. I don't think my sister ever fully recovered from that. It sounds brutal, but these rituals meant so much to our aunts – they truly believed they were doing good and healing our souls. Over forty years later, both Nicole and I still carry with us a sense of fear about our spiritual cleanliness.

◆

Honouring the dead and observing rituals relating to the afterlife were a badge of honour for my Italian family, perhaps because life on the islands was so harsh and, especially after the war, death was too common. Or perhaps it was just a fear of God that held them to account. I remember regular visits to one of my zias, who would bring out her funeral shroud every time we arrived. It was basically a cheap blue nightgown featuring a huge picture of the Virgin Mary. It kind of stressed me out that she was going to be buried in something so gaudy. But she was so happy and proud of it that I played along. She would lay it out on the table so we could inspect it and we would 'ooooh' and 'aaahh' and say how beautiful it was. Mostly, I was thinking about performing for the tiramisu cake reward after it was all over. She had good tiramisu cake at her house. She was definitely nearing the end of her time on earth, so I guess this was her way of coping with that reality. She didn't know what would take her from this life, so at least she could control her clothing. Something about that weird blue funeral shroud really seemed to bring her comfort.

I heard a secret whisper among the adults that the funeral-shroud-obsessed zia shared a love child with my nonno. This made the cynic in me wonder if the whole routine of showing the shroud to us was done just to curry sympathy. I don't know if Nonna was aware of the rumours. If she was, she never let on. I believed that my nonna was a heavenly angel who walked the earth, so the thought of someone doing her wrong stoked the fires of retribution in my Sicilian soul and part of my heart savoured the idea of this woman spending eternity in a hideous polyester frock. On the other hand, these were just gossipy whispers and she seemed like a fairly harmless old lady, so I tried not to give it too much thought.

This focus on death and the afterlife was slowly and surely feeding an obsession I was developing with my own mortality, but since these things were always approached with the essence of deep emotion or celebration and joy, I didn't really know how it affected me until I got older. Unfortunately, by then, the seeds were well and truly sown.

◆

My childhood wasn't *all* dabbling in exorcisms followed by excellent Italian food. The other half of my family was as Aussie as they come. I had Nanna and Grandfather, of course, and my mum's sister was pure country. She lived in the remote town of Charlton, between Melbourne and Mildura, with her six kids, who were all awesome. Visits to their place were always filled with adventure. My cousins would rough and tumble with me, and my aunty would let us wander around like free-range chickens and have as much fun as we liked. It was pure joy.

One visit, in the middle of a terrible mouse plague, the adults put me to bed on a mattress on the floor encircled by mousetraps and told that if I needed to go to the toilet, I should probably wait until morning. 'Goodnight, love.'

All I heard once the lights went out was *Snap! Snap! Snap!*
A bit gruesome, but it was good training for a future
Survivor player.

I loved my early years in Melbourne, pinballing between
my very Italian side and my very Australian side. In true
Gemini style, I often felt split down the middle, but it
was a feeling that I cherished even though it left me a
bit confused. I consider one major lucky break in my life
was the blessing of amazing grandparents. I inherited my
nonna's passion for food and mystery and, I like to think,
her resilience. And if I have a flair for fashion it definitely
comes from my nanna, who knew how to put together a
twin-set and did her hair in rollers every morning so that
she always looked like an old-school movie star. I inherited
a passion for neatness and cleaning from Nanna too; she
loved a freshly vacuumed carpet and the smell of Mr
Sheen, both things that still give me great joy. She was so
organised that when my cousin Anthony came down from
the country to live with her, she would religiously dust
and neaten his massive stack of chronologically displayed
Penthouse magazines that lined the wall of his room, no
questions asked. As long as they weren't dusty then they
couldn't offend anyone.

My grandfather was great fun and when I was at his
and Nanna's place, I would spend a lot of time with him
watching our beloved Bloods play AFL. (Like all true Bloods

fans, when South Melbourne Football Club became the Sydney Swans, my family stayed loyal.) Grandfather tried to get me into cricket too, but it bored me senseless. He'd occasionally sneak me swigs of his Melbourne Bitter longneck while we cheered the Bloods on, which possibly gave me a predilection for alcohol at way too young an age, but it was the 1980s and that's how things were back then.

Grandfather would occasionally take me to an AFL game and I guess that's how I fell in love with football. We would sit in the stands together, me munching on a pie while he drank a beer, and get completely raucous, screaming and yelling when we kicked a goal. During every football outing he'd share with me the 'secret' that he was friends with the umpire and had told them his granddaughter was coming to the game that day, so they had agreed to help us win. Whenever the Swans were awarded a free kick he would say, 'Did you see the umpire wink at us? That free kick was for you!' I would sit up straight in my seat completely chuffed and full of pride knowing I was the secret ingredient for a Swans victory. I actually believed this story until my early twenties, which in hindsight seems naive, but I loved those times so much, I didn't want to let go of the magic.

Around this time I began to develop health anxieties; the fact that *Quincy M.E.* was my favourite TV show probably didn't help. *Quincy* was a great show starring Jack Klugman as a medical examiner who helped the LAPD investigate mysterious deaths. Mum and I loved it – we would snuggle on the couch with some Milo and ice cream and watch it together, but I was harbouring a secret. I would study those mysterious deaths and then add them to the Rolodex in my brain of possible disasters that may befall me. I would run into my bedroom during the commercial breaks just to test that my heart was still beating, and if I couldn't find a pulse then a jolt of fear would burst through my body. Luckily, this would cause my heartbeat to go into overdrive and, panicked but relieved, I'd inevitably be able to locate it and return to the couch, satisfied I would live to see another day.

◆

Outside of being with my family, most of my spare time was filled with ballet, reading books and watching old musicals – but mostly ballet. After my Aunty Rosslyn let me start dancing at The Charlesworth School of Dance following my two-year-old tantrum, I spent most of my early years there, so I had access to as many classes as I liked. I wanted to become a professional ballerina pretty much instantly. For most of my childhood I danced around the house all day, daydreaming of being on stage with Baryshnikov or Nureyev. I was happiest when I was alone in my room or in the lounge room, doing ballet or making up plays. I always wanted to be somewhere else, somewhere magical, and so I taught myself to disappear into my own head and live in an alternate reality. At some point in about second grade, a rumour followed me around that some bigwig from London had seen me dance and they'd said I was the best ballerina of my age in the world. Something like that definitely did happen but full disclosure: I am pretty sure I took some creative license with it and probably asked Nicole to spread the story around school. However it happened, it stuck and I actually began to believe it.

I couldn't, however, shake the feeling that something was up, that some dark, terrible event was coming for me. I was convinced that our house was haunted and that the only way to stop the ghost killing me in the night was to rinse my mouth out seven times after brushing my teeth, lift my legs up at exactly the same time when I hopped into bed and say one Our Father and a Hail Mary lying in bed while facing the open door. We lived in a big old house on Tooronga Road in Malvern with ornate red velvet wallpaper adorning the walls and a long dark hallway that I used to sneak down multiple times at night to jump into my parents bed, hoping they wouldn't notice. They always did and I was promptly taken back to my room, where I would lie in bed, paralysed, waiting for the ghost with his flowing hair and snarling face to come and torture me.

I was a hyperactive, happy-go-lucky child on the outside. On the inside, I was often fighting to push through feelings of fear and confusion. I'm not sure why all of these things consumed my tiny brain, but my consciousness was over-whelmed by fantasies that I confused with reality. I was still mostly upbeat though because when I entered the ballet studio the clouds would part and the world would shine. I loved walking in and seeing the pianist in the corner of the room ready to bang out the tunes for our class on the old wooden piano. I loved seeing my friends and the smell of Cedel hairspray and the leotards and mirrors and most of all I loved tying the ribbons perfectly on my little pink ballet shoes. It all made me so happy and I truly believed that God had put me on this earth for the sole purpose of being the world's greatest prima ballerina. I was obviously wrong, but I didn't know that yet.

I started to shape my identity around my balletic talent and it influenced how I saw myself, which, at the time, felt great. I was so happy, driven and filled with purpose and I felt loved, which soothed my soul. I was still in early primary school, though, so I was too young to realise what goes up must come down, and often with a thud. The rollercoaster of emotions would be a regular theme in my life, but for now I was up. Well up.

CHAPTER FOUR

Who leaves – their own comfort zone – succeeds!
SICILIAN PROVERB

When I was in Year 3, my dad was looking for new opportunities. Like his father, he always wanted to do the best for his family, but I think he also wanted adventure and he wasn't afraid to change things up. I don't remember being told that we were moving to Darwin, but I remember it feeling sudden and scary. I didn't want to leave Melbourne, I was happy.

Dad worked in retail and had been offered a job managing Casuarina shopping centre, which we all understood was a big opportunity for him. My mum has always been a medical secretary and so her work would be easy to transfer to a new place. I'm not sure that she was thrilled about moving. I loved visiting my mum at the doctors' office and helping her do the filing. I found filing bizarrely thrilling actually; I still do – I guess it feeds my love for organisation in a world that seems so messy.

I don't ever remember my parents fighting, but I could always tell when there was silent tension brewing, and the impending move to Darwin seemed like one of those times. I was only seven though so I may have misinterpreted my own trepidation for family stress. I knew that I was really unhappy about leaving my grandparents. I was also pretty sad about leaving my friends behind, even though they never let me be the blonde one when we played ABBA.

So, out of the blue, we packed up and moved. It was a huge culture shift and a long way from Melbourne. We were headed into an unfamiliar environment, one that would shape my childhood in the most lovely way. I remember the moment I stepped off the plane, being hit in the face by the hot thick air. I was so used to the cool Melbourne weather, I wondered how I was going to survive and, more importantly, how I was going to dance in that heat. I was pleasantly surprised by how quickly I adapted to my new life up north. The beach, the sunsets, the house with a pool – it really was enchanting. My new school was a friendly place and there was so much to do outdoors in my spare time, which was a huge contrast to Melbourne, where we spent so much of the year inside hiding from the cold. I very quickly went from being a sheltered city mouse to appreciating the pleasure of picking the green bums off the ants that ran around on the pavement and eating them for a snack at recess. (If you know, you know – they taste like honey.) I had a pet blue-tongue lizard that lived in my backyard and I would make houses out of shoeboxes on our verandah for geckos to hang out in, which they hated. I tried mangrove worms, played double-dutch with my new friends at school and I finally learnt to swim. As I entered a new 'worship the big kids' phase I spent a lot of spare time hanging out barefoot in the sun with my sister and her friends.

There was so much I loved about Darwin at that time; everything felt free and happy. I experienced for the first time Darwin's annual Beer Can Regatta, where people created boats out of empty beer cans and then raced them on the water. The beer can race and the thong-throwing contest were my favourite activities at the regatta. There were so many fun events up there and I even entered my beloved pet frog in a Frogalympics competition – unfortunately he bounced the wrong way and ended up getting lost. RIP Kermit.

Darwin was an excellent fit for me. I was tanned and energised and had no regrets about our move. My dad was loving Darwin too. He bought a second fridge exclusively for beer and cans of Tab, he took up barramundi fishing and most weekends he roamed around in his 'Ted Egan's bloody good drinkers club' t-shirt, which was comically offset by his thick Italian moustache and gold jewellery.

Nicole had started high school and I quickly worked out that it was a more difficult place to navigate than primary school. She often came home upset and would talk about the bullying and racial tension at school. She was old enough to understand the social issues that were going on around her. On top of that there weren't many Italian kids in Darwin so she was labelled the 'wog girl'. Back then being a 'wog' was anything but cool; we were called 'slimy' and 'greasy' and some people thought we all smelled like salami, which at the time was still a weird delicacy that not many people had tried. Obviously salami is king, but this was the golden era of devon and Strasburg so we were outnumbered.

I was at a Catholic primary school, so there was a lot of focus for the Catholic students on preparing for our First Holy Communion. I was so excited by this because my back-up plan if I didn't make it as a ballet dancer was to be a nun. Sister Helen had already taken me under her wing and was guiding me toward light, so I was all-in for this Communion caper. When I put my mind to something, I give it my all so I studied hard, listened and nailed my Communion with flying colours. My back-up career as a nun was cemented in stone.

My nonna and nanna and grandfather all came up for the big day, and I was so proud of my white dress and veil that I refused to take off my outfit for bed. I slept in it, happily knowing that God was so pleased with me.

◆

My time in Darwin was sprinkled with good memories and adventure. I had my ninth birthday up there: a pool party where my friends and I put on costume makeup and re-enacted Old Hollywood sychronised swimming for hours. I was loving ballet, and as I grew older, it started to edge out playing with lizards or swimming in the pool as my favourite pastime.

My obsession with books and movies was also really kicking off, and I began to wonder whether I might try my hand at acting. Just as this was formulating in my mind, my twelve-year-old sister was scouted by a film producer at a ballet recital and before we knew it, she was packed off to Melbourne to star in a movie. I was pretty thrilled that I was about to have a famous sister and I was hoping the same thing might happen to me.

The movie Nicole was cast in was called *Moving Out* about a young Italian family in inner-city Melbourne. It starred Vince Colosimo and is a beautiful, classic coming-of-age film about the Italian migrant experience in the eighties. I was so proud of her and thought she was so cool. It was then that I decided I wanted to be in movies too. A dancing nun who starred in films? I could make that work.

◆

Nicole went to live with our grandparents while she was shooting in Melbourne, and I felt my sister's absence overwhelmingly in the evenings. She used to humour me with little repetitive routines before bed, where we would say the same thing back and forth to each other before we went to sleep. Without that reassuring habit I found it hard to settle and insomnia started to descend on me.

I would lie in bed, worrying about something bad happening. It was an abstract feeling, but I also couldn't shake the terror or the notion that I was floating in space with no anchor and the only end was death. So I prayed and prayed. It didn't help. I would stare into the abyss until the early hours of the morning, trying to invoke the vision of Mary because I felt if she came to me then all would be okay. The words of my zias would come back to me and I was consumed with the idea that I might be a visionary, which would prove that God was definitely real and therefore I could stop worrying about the afterlife. After hours of waiting for her to come to me each night, I started to create new habitual ceremonies, hoping that they would bring me good fortune and curry favour with the Holy Spirit.

I had flirted with these rituals back when I was warding off ghosts in Tooronga Road, but Darwin was when I really committed to it. Washing out my mouth seven times after brushing my teeth, seven signs of the cross, two Hail Marys, knocking on the wall seven times. The number seven got a big run in those days. These practices became longer and more elaborate as the years went on. I would repeat them over and over, and I guess it was some sort of childhood obsessive-compulsive behaviour, but to me they were protective rituals to please the spirits and keep me safe. Sometimes at night I would beg God to tell me that everything was in place, and I was convinced I heard him say yes so I took comfort in that. I kept adding to my nightly routines, which always ended with a quick prayer. Usually Glory Be. Eventually they would get too long, so I would go cold turkey for a week or two until I started them up again and the game would continue.

I found the hum of the television comforting so I would try to fall asleep before my parents went to bed, but I rarely managed it, leaving just me, the darkness and the silence. Sometimes I wonder if all of this unfocused fear was the realisation that life is like being on a train with an unknown destination, and I just hadn't yet worked out that I shouldn't worry about where it was going to stop.

CHAPTER FIVE

Those who sing through the summer
must dance in the winter.
ITALIAN SAYING

Turns out, that train did stop and, in a surprisingly banal turn of events, the destination happened to be Canberra. After only two years in Darwin came another move away from friends, and it was all out of my control. But the upside of moving as a kid is that you can reinvent yourself and meet people who haven't experienced your awkward and terrible moments. Being four years older than me, Nicole had to head straight to middle high school, which must have been hard. I never asked her about it because I was too deep in my own makeover story. She seemed popular and happy, though, so I think Canberra was a good fit for her. I saw this move as a bold opportunity to create a new character and leave behind the things about myself that were boring. I could make a new start, reinvent myself. That sounded fun. I was nine years old and I was about to start Year 4 so I thought the most appropriate way to approach this was to change my personality, my clothes, my voice and, well, basically everything. I wanted to add some excitement to my life and I was convinced that this was the best way to do it. I had been watching *The Brady Bunch* a lot in the afternoons so I decided that an American accent would be the obvious way to win friends and influence people, although I hadn't thought of a backstory to give this any authenticity. I just hoped nobody would dig too deep.

My hair was another thing I decided to change. I thought two low pigtails and a thick ballet headband would be a good combination. It seemed suitably American, and Marcia Brady would totally pull off that look, so why wouldn't I? I even begged Mum to teach me how to make a pecan pie so I could seem more authentic. I was fairly confident that these changes would make me very popular so I was pumped to unleash the new me.

On the first day at Sts Peter & Paul's Primary School I remember standing alone in the Year 4 classroom feeling appropriately uncertain about the pigtails and headband I'd chosen when a girl with a big ribbon in her hair bounced in. She flashed me a thousand-watt smile and said, 'Hi I'm Katherine!'

I was taken aback as I was expecting the usual new-kid awkward start; this friendliness immediately demolished my defences. 'Hi, I'm Pia!' I responded in an Australian accent. *Oh, dammit!* Katherine asked me lots of questions about who I was and where I came from and I chatted away without a care in the world. She was so charismatic and interesting that I forgot about my alias, slowly pulled off the headband and returned to what I thought was my less-impressive true self. But Katherine seemed dazzled with me just as I was. We discovered our birthdays were two days apart and immediately decided we should have a joint party. I was having one of those rare moments in life when you meet someone special.

◆

The principal of my new school in Canberra was a tough old nun who really didn't seem to like me much. This shook me to my core and completely turned me off the idea of joining the nunnery. I just seemed to grind her gears and I was never sure why, but I was such a boisterous child I could have that effect on people sometimes. This was probably a good thing because in hindsight I would probably have tried to live out some Colleen McCullough *Thorn Birds*–inspired fantasy and end up being kicked out of the church. Although, I still think I would have made a very cool nun.

I was an intense observer of people and I would often quietly ponder who they were and what made them tick.

I could be a shapeshifter, shaping my reactions and conversations to fit into the moment I was in. I'd collect personality traits and idiosyncrasies from other people that I would later use myself – something that was helpful when I started acting. Sometimes I think this came from moving schools, other times I think it might just be an odd hobby. This practice led me to realise that sometimes our lives are shaped by the struggles of others and often the heroes we observe are oblivious to the fact that they are having an effect on those around them. Watching someone stay upright in a world that is trying to beat them down can shape us forever. I'm constantly amazed by how strong people can be in the face of trauma. My nonna was one such person and, though I didn't know it, I was about to encounter at close hand the same kind of perseverance in two others.

One was a woman I never met and the other was my mother.

◆

I always wanted to meet Gay Davidson because she was kind of famous. I knew her daughter, Kiri, from ballet school and I was desperate for us to be sleepover-become-part-of-the-family kind of friends. My new ballet school was so competitive and one that you only attended if you were very serious about dance. It had a reputation for being a blue-ribbon school and was known for encouraging a strict work ethic. The training was vigorous and the pressure to succeed was fierce, but I was young, ambitious and had the drive of an athlete so I coped fine. There was to my mind, however, something missing in the culture of the school. It always felt cold and soulless and it was a cutthroat environment. Ballet to me has always been about passion and storytelling. Sure, technique is critical, but dance is about love and emotion. Unfortunately I didn't feel encouraged and the atmosphere didn't feel friendly, and so sometimes it was hard to pour myself into my tight black leotard on those cold Canberra nights.

I'd always shared a special bond with my ballet friends because we were untethered from the social stresses of school and bonded by passion and hard work. I wanted to share that bond with Kiri.

Kiri looked like the popular girl in every high school movie. She had a thick long mane of blonde hair that she wore in a high ponytail, which would swing happily from side to side when she walked. She was bouncy and fun and would always leap up on the bench in the dressing-room and hold court for her adoring admirers, of which I was one. She had just the right amount of humour and wit to make her incredibly disarming. She would loudly exclaim 'same' when she was in agreement with you. Kiri had all the qualifications to be a mean girl, but she was so nice and friendly.

Around this time my moustache and leg hair was doing a nice job of settling in and I was jealous of my fair-haired friends who didn't have to worry about such hirsute intrusions. I liked to hang around them in the hope that some of their blonde goddess fairy dust would rub off on me. Kiri was one of those goddesses, and everything I wanted to be, so I was meticulously planning out a sleepover in my head. Sleepovers were how you made things official as besties and I could tell that in no time we would be having midnight snacks and dancing to Bananarama in her bedroom. Kiri was definitely my favourite person at ballet and I would look forward to seeing her as she filled those pre-class dressing-room hangouts with energy. I even started saying 'same' all the time to friends at school. I still say it sometimes.

If it wasn't enough that Kiri was so charismatic and charming, her mum was quite a big deal in Canberra at the time too. In the 1970s Gay Davidson became a political correspondent for the *Canberra Times*, the first woman in Australia to do so for a major newspaper. In 1985 she became the first female president of the National Press Club. She was a true trailblazer. In addition to her intelligence and literary talent she gained notoriety because, noticing the lack of accessible female amenities in the Canberra Press Gallery, Gay began stubbornly using the men's toilets and encouraging her female counterparts to do the same. Because of her persistence, the toilets were eventually changed to unisex. She was constantly winning battles in a world dominated by men. She a pioneer and I would learn later that she was also a fierce supporter and mentor of young female reporters who were starting out. She was known for her wisdom, being a natural teacher and as the kind of person who would lift up those who surrounded her. Gay had a popular column in the *Canberra Times*, where she demonstrated her insightful commentary and opinions on social issues. In 1980s Canberra, she was an important person and historically she still is.

I never met Gay because I never got that sleepover. And the reason why was the moment I first felt the magic of young childhood disappear.

◆

Around the same time that I was dealing with all the changes my body was going through, I could feel the world shifting around me again. My anxiety had abated a little after moving from Darwin, but all of a sudden it was sneaking back in. I probably had hormones to thank for that. I still didn't have the word 'anxiety' in my vocabulary, I just interpreted how I felt as a divine premonition that something terrible was about to happen. In my final year of primary school, I could definitely feel change in the air. But there was also a lot of fun to be had and, fortunately or unfortunately, I started to get into some mischief.

The call of the nunnery started to fade at the same time as I began to have my first taste of how exhilarating being a tiny bit naughty could be. I was all-in for some nonsense as long as I didn't get caught. I was never the ringleader, but if you wanted a faithful apostle on your journey to hell, I would follow you to the end. (I kind of still will.) Luckily I had just the right sprinkling of study nerd to keep me out of *too* much trouble, but I definitely inherited my father's appreciation for hilarious mischievousness.

One of the things girls at my school were subjected to (not by the nuns, thank God) was weekly 'frigid tests' in the playground. And it wasn't just our school, it was an epidemic that we misinterpreted as an unwelcome rite of passage. The boys would run a finger from the top of your head down your body and if you flinched you were teased for being frigid for the rest of the week. I wasn't sure what frigid was and for a while there I wondered if it had something to do with a fridge, but I shut my eyes and suffered the tests just to get some peace. There were 'scrag fights' too, and stolen cigarettes were smoked in the bushes before school. I went along with it all, only pretending to smoke because I thought it tasted terrible and I was too much of a hypochondriac to risk cancer. I faked it because it was what the cool kids were doing and I liked the silly routine of spraying Impulse all over our uniforms afterwards so that we didn't get caught.

The teachers at my primary school always seemed grumpy. I think that was just a result of the time we lived in rather than my school being particularly terrible. I didn't hate school and I would always strive for good grades, but I felt impatient with the system and the people who ran it. I know my dad helped establish that kind of attitude as he left school at a young age and openly valued hard work over education. My father, like his father, Salvatore, had a mild distaste for any authority, which was partly due to his volcanic spirit, but I think it also stemmed from the racial abuse he suffered during his school years. Dad had a feisty attitude wrapped up in a tough exterior and though it often felt like he was sticking up his middle finger to the world, he did it with enough charisma and humour that he got away with it. I inherited some of those traits, which have served me well at times and unfortunately failed me at others.

Just as school was starting to lose its sparkle, ballet began doing the same. I still wanted to be a ballerina, but most of the time I preferred to stay home and read because I had an insatiable appetite for stories. I loved *The Neverending Story*, Judy Blume and Trixie Belden and eventually I inherited my sister's delightfully disturbing Virginia Andrews novels at way too young an age. I just wanted to be curled in my room with Pixie my cat and my books for hours at a time.

◆

I think my desperation for solitude was intensified by the fact that I wasn't loving my new ballet school. Ballet had always been my safe space, but I started to dread going. I would much rather stay home with *Flowers in the Attic* and dance my own choreography in the lounge room. I had the sinking feeling that the competition I was up against was getting fiercer and the fear of not being the best was crushing.

So many of us were ambitious and the realisation that only a few of us would make it meant that we were all looking for a way to push ourselves to the front of the pack. This is a lot for a bunch of twelve-year-olds to digest. We were too young to understand the gravity of these feelings; we deeply cared for each other, even though we were also hoping to leave everyone else eating our dust. Negative food talk really started to escalate in the dressing-rooms – all of our bodies were starting to grow and change and this can be hard to embrace as a dancer.

I was not alone in noticing that it was the older girls with long graceful limbs who seemed to get the lead roles and accolades, and I wanted to be one of them. They were often pale and pretty with elegant features and an air of confidence that came with being blessed aesthetically. I didn't want to be the little 'wog' chick who liked eating eggplant. I wanted to be an 'Amy' or a 'Chloe', which was unfortunately a phase I struggled to grow out of for a long time. Most of us had some form of self-criticism about our bodies so we would discuss these in the dressing-room and share stories about how to stay thin and stave off the lumpy downfalls of puberty.

One day before class my friend brought in a box of chocolates and we all practised unwrapping each treat, chewing it slowly so that some of the delicious juices trickled into the back of our throats, then spitting the chocolate back into the wrapper before swallowing. It was ostensibly a tutorial in how to taste chocolate without the calories, but what I was really receiving was my first lesson in how to treat food like the enemy. It was a lot to digest, or not digest, but those messages would come in thick and fast for many years.

◆

Kiri was a shining light at that ballet school, with a natural talent as a dancer. But then, I started to notice her absence a lot – she wasn't the constant that she been.

turn up to class, she was still entertaining and kind, but then she would go missing again and it would be another week until she returned and brightened up my day. But even that routine started to change. Something had altered in Kiri, although I couldn't put my finger on what it was. She just wasn't her bright self anymore. We didn't chat like we used to, and she seemed a bit lost, almost like a shy new kid. Something was off and I started to sense doom, although that wasn't unusual for me.

Class was silent and strict and you had to be on your game or you would be pulled up for your laziness and lack of commitment. Most of us found this teaching style helped push us to excel, but in Kiri's case the criticism started to feel misguided. Her dancing wasn't the same and she was getting confused doing the simplest routines, so the teacher was calling her out a lot.

After a particularly long absence from classes, Kiri returned. I was so happy to see her again and I was hoping she was back to her old self, but it was quickly apparent that she wasn't. The thing about kids is that sometimes they know or feel things that adults miss because their minds aren't congested with the complications of life. I knew that day that something was really wrong.

Kiri and I took our usual places next to each other on the floor. We were in the second row, which was a good place to be because you could hide behind the other girls and hopefully stray out of the teacher's eyeline. It didn't help. The teacher zeroed in on Kiri, screaming her name over and over, 'Kiri, what are you doing? Kiri, keep up!' She was really mad. I looked at Kiri and I saw her tapping her right foot up and down on the spot, trying to perform a simple *rond de jambe*, but seemingly unable to make sense of her body. She was staring at her foot and staring at me, her eyes begging for help. I didn't know what I could do. We had been groomed to have an overwhelming fear of the teacher's wrath and, right then, we were just trying to survive the hour. The more the teacher yelled, the more confused Kiri became and I could tell she couldn't remember the routine. In fact, it looked like she couldn't remember how to dance at all.

'It's going to be okay, just copy me,' I said. Eventually the teacher worked out something was wrong too, and she left us alone. Kiri and I entered our own little world and she slowly tried to follow my steps. I encouraged her, but a light had gone out in her eyes. I remember my face was hot and my stomach was churning. I tried to be brave for her because she seemed to be bolstered by my support. I don't recall how the class ended, but I do remember that it was the last time I saw Kiri. I have a terrible feeling that I didn't say goodbye and that I rushed out of there, flustered and desperate to get home, where I would feel safe. I carried around guilt about that for years – why didn't I say goodbye?

Soon after that class Mum sat me down and told me Kiri was sick and not able to have any visitors. She died not long after that of something called sub-acute sclerosing panencephalitis, a progressive neurological disorder which affects young people who have been infected by the measles virus, usually before they are two years old. It is some sort of overreaction to the virus, and its progression is slow and devastating.

When I was researching for this book I found an old article that Gay wrote for the *Canberra Times* about the tragedy of losing her daughter. She said the first sign something was wrong was when Kiri's grades started slipping, then it started to affect her socially. She described how Kiri lost friends as they found her aggressive and bossy. She then started acting obsessively, lost her co-ordination and eventually began twitching and jerking, which she would try to cover up. It took a long time for her to be diagnosed but, once she was, the prognosis was brutal and final.

Sometimes people can turn grief into action and Gay was definitely a woman of action, so she went on a tireless campaign to promote the measles vaccine in Australia. She would pop up on TV using her journalistic experience and her profile to spread her message and Mum would call me into the lounge room, 'Kiri's mum is on TV!' I would run in to get a glimpse of the famous reporter, who I never had the chance to meet.

CHAPTER SIX

*Whoever decides to change is aware of not
knowing what the change may bring.*

SICILIAN PROVERB

The death of Kiri was something I absorbed, but didn't
dwell on in daylight hours. I was finally in high school and
was turning thirteen, which supplied adequate distractions
from life traumas. High school was fun, Katherine was
with me and we were having a fairly good time in our
new school, St Clare's College. Soon, however, I would
have another lesson in the arbitrariness of life and how
its difficulties could be faced with astounding grace and
determination.

Mum always looked good; she had a gorgeous mane of
silky chestnut-coloured hair that she wore in a bob with
a fringe. It was super chic and suited her classic style.
She also had a great love and appreciation for fashion,
and always looked well turned out. A love of shopping and

clothes was something she passed on to me, and we would travel to Melbourne twice a year to do a massive seasonal wardrobe refresh. I loved those trips more than Christmas. I remember around this time buying a pair of moon boots (google them!) and a navy corduroy miniskirt that I would team with a hot pink jumper. My second favourite outfit was a grey matching tracksuit where the pants had a built-in frilly miniskirt. I was clearly nailing it. Mum and Nanna were very nifty with a sewing machine as well, which was handy when making ballet costumes, as every sequin would have to be individually stitched on, every hem sewn to perfection. We had a collective passion for fashion.

Mum was as energetic as ever so I didn't know that there was anything wrong because she didn't mention it to me. Then, sometime when I was in Year 7, she went in to hospital to have a hysterectomy. From what I could tell, the issues she'd been having were debilitating and she was looking forward to feeling like her old self. I remember being pulled out of class to find Dad waiting for me. He told me that the operation had gone okay and that Mum was going to be better now. I hadn't really known that it was such a big deal until that moment, but I felt happy that he seemed relieved.

When Mum came home from the hospital things seemed different, heavy, and I was definitely not prepared for it. She seemed distracted and would constantly run her hands through her hair looking for something in between her fingers. It was a repetitive action that was more often than not followed by a soft distressed sigh as she looked at her hand. I don't remember being told that she had alopecia, but I came to understand that her hair was falling out and it seemed to be happening fast. It was like watching someone on a runaway train – you knew they couldn't get off and even worse, you couldn't help. Alopecia is often triggered by trauma or stress and it seemed that the operation had flicked a switch that was causing her body to attack her hair follicles, exposing large patches of her scalp.

I became an expert at playing patch detective for Mum. I would inspect her head and report whether I saw any new hair growing (I didn't) or if the patches were getting bigger (they were). I would try to be positive and suggest that perhaps I saw some new fluff or that maybe the patch was smaller, but it was just my mind playing tricks on me because I felt a sense of responsibility to make things better. Mum tried everything: a holiday, knitting, trips to a doctor in Sydney who would paint her head in a substance that made her skin seep yellow liquid and peel off. No matter what she did, the hair kept falling.

I watched it all unfold quietly and solemnly, and when I heard someone mention the word 'genetic' I grappled with a deep sense of fear that this was coming for me too. I didn't want to be angry, but I was. I really liked Mum's hair and I hated watching this happen to her. But I could be careless with my words too. I remember once loudly complaining in front of company about hair being in my dinner 'again'. Mum left the room and burst into tears. Looking back, she tells me, 'The loss of control over what was happening to my body was frightening. I tried to stay upbeat externally but internally I was falling apart.' I felt so awful and embarrassed by what I'd blurted out – it was the first time I remember seeing Mum as a human being and not just my mother. I never mentioned hair in my dinner again, but before long there was none left to fall out anyway.

Every hair on her body slowly fell out. Now Mum jokes that the only hair that survived was the hair on her toes – 'One of God's little jokes.' When it was all gone, it seemed like there was nothing left to fear because the worst had happened and she was still standing. I kept doing the head checks looking for fluff, which I occasionally spotted, but for the most part Mum remained hairless. She was reborn.

Being a woman of style she picked herself up and created a whole new look for herself. She had an inner resolve, and although I didn't express it at the time, I was inspired by her tenacity – I wasn't sure I possessed that level of courage. She seemed to accept her new appearance and became a master at drawing on feathery natural eyebrows and experimenting with lashes and makeup to enhance her eyes. She bought a wig that was a gorgeous bob with bangs in a chestnut brown that made her look like her old self. It was the loss of her eyebrows and lashes, she said, that really made life hard. Turns out they are there for a reason and without them, Mum's eyes were constantly irritated by sweat and dust. She always rushed to put a wig or scarf on when my friends came over. I'm not sure if it was for her or them, but before long it became the new normal.

My sister and I didn't talk too much about it at the time, but we were bonded by the experience of being helpless witnesses. Nicole's life was busy being her best teenage self with big teased hair and heavy makeup that complimented her flashy clothes and spray-on jeans. She was nailing the hot 1980s Italian-girl look and she elevated it by hanging with edgy friends whose piercings and shaved undercuts seemed so cool to me. I dressed in sporty shorts and t-shirts most days so I was captivated by my sister's dazzling appearance, though I knew I could never pull that off. Boys liked her too – she had boyfriends with cars and was always going out and would come home and tell me about it all afterwards. I found it endlessly fascinating.

I learnt everything I needed to know from my sister – no awkward parental talks required for me. She would warn me about boys, and, to be honest, I avoided them romantically for a very long time, mostly because I really wasn't interested. When I finally had my first kiss at thirteen (with a boy called Luke), I didn't really like it because he kissed too hard and it kind of hurt, so I stayed away from boys for a while and lived vicariously through my sister's romances. I kissed a girl too, which I quite liked, but that stuff was literally kept in the closet back in those days – let me tell you, the sports utilities closet at my Catholic primary school saw quite a bit of action between the Year 6 ladies. I was a slow burn when it came to romantic interests because I was too focused on ballet, too busy and the thought of leaving childhood behind was wildly unappealing to me. It was all pretty normal 'growing up in the eighties' stuff.

When Nicole and I spoke about Mum's alopecia it was because we were young, confused and a bit scared. We both feared losing our hair; it was something that hung over our heads (pun intended) every time we went to get a haircut. I knew Nicole was afraid, but I had an intuition that she would be fine and it was only coming for me.

Mum soldiered on – she was determined to regain her lashes and brows, and even though it is rare to do so with alopecia universalis, after some time she eventually did. To this day the hair on her head continues to sporadically come and go in fluffy patches, but the fluff helps her wigs stay in place, so she is satisfied with that. She still rocks her wigs, although the bob with bangs was retired a few years ago and now she is a shaggy blonde, still embracing style in her seventies.

I wish I could say that when I was younger I used the experience of Mum dealing with alopecia to better understand the pressures of living with physical differences, but I'm ashamed to say that I didn't. I was still so influenced by magazines, advertising and television and what was defined by them as beautiful. I packed any lessons I learnt tightly inside my brain and every night in bed ran my fingers through my hair, looking for strands that had fallen out. If I counted more than seven, I panicked because I wasn't sure that I would cope if I developed alopecia. The odd thing is, years later it did come for me, though in a different form, and what I learnt then was that the thing I feared the most was actually exactly what I needed in order to change my perspective. But I still had years ahead of me before that; years that I would waste trying to fit into a cutthroat world where physical perfection was everything. Rather than question that environment, I questioned myself for not being pretty enough to please those who oversaw it. If only I could go back knowing what I know now.

CHAPTER SEVEN

A friend is the one who knows everything about
you and yet continues to be your friend.

ITALIAN SAYING

As hair remained a constant theme and my journey through high school continued, I decided I needed my own transformation. Goodbye bob with bangs . . . it was time to get a body wave! For those of you too young to know what a body wave is, it is a loose, wavy perm that was very popular in the 1980s. Watch *Desperately Seeking Susan*: Madonna's hair is what a great body wave looks like. Katherine had one and I wanted one too.

A body wave was also known as a perm for wimps. It gives your hair a nice wavy style that you can ruin by scrunch-drying it with criminal amounts of mousse so that it's hard, sticky and doesn't move for the whole day. All the cool girls had them and I was desperate for one so Mum took me to the hairdresser and paid for my first major makeover. That was the good thing about my mum, she was always supportive of a style update even if it hurt the wallet. So off I went, oblivious to the fact that a perm probably wasn't the right choice for a half-Italian girl with a moustache and caterpillars for eyebrows. I didn't care, I've always loved a trend.

I adored my body wave; and Katherine and I would team them with huge ribbons that we would fashion as a headband and then tie in a big bow. Matching outfits were everything back then. My favourite look was a hot pink-and-white polo shirt from Sportsgirl, homemade acid-wash jeans that I had bleached in the bath, and a big, oversized bow on the side of my head. We can talk about the gold balloon skirt with fishnets that I wore to the Year 9 blue light disco later. Right at this moment I felt like I was nailing it (which in hindsight I'm not sure I was); I was aiming to be a preppy fashion icon and the body wave was the icing on the cake. I was loving my slightly quirky 1980s fashion vibe and before long an off-the-shoulder t-shirt and hot pink rollerskates were my new off-duty uniform. I had changed ballet schools and I was actually enjoying high school. It was happy times ahead.

The Dell Brady School of Ballet in Canberra was everything I had hoped for; strict in the best possible way, but also caring, fun and passionate. I started to feel like my old self again and I didn't dread going to class anymore.

Saturdays at my new school were long and exhausting, but I loved them and we became a close family of girls who enjoyed dancing together all day long. We did tap, character, jazz and, of course, my number one love, ballet. I wanted to be the best ballet dancer in the world, just like I thought I was when I was six. Sometimes our bodies aren't built for the glory that we have planned for them, but I hadn't twigged to that yet and I was being blindly led by my drive and passion. Life would eventually teach me that you have to accept your limitations and be content with the opportunities that come your way.

Dell Brady was where I met Rachel Rawlins. Rachel had a sweet, measured personality and a body that was built to dance. I was good, but she was amazing. Rumours started to swirl about her, that she had a studio in her house, that she practised at home until midnight every night, that someone had spotted her eating a whole Cherry Ripe at the shops! God forbid. I'd never seen anyone dance as well as Rachel did and although we started as equals it wasn't long before she surpassed me in skill and performance. Some of the girls liked to talk about Rachel behind her back, for no reason other than jealousy. It was my first taste of how futile jealousy really is. It seemed like they thought that if they cut her down a little perhaps she wouldn't dance as well, but that's not how the world works. When someone is great at something they will stay great no matter what you say about them; saying horrible shit just eats you up inside, so there is no point.

Rachel was really nice, so I tried to stay away from the nonsense and curb my fantasies about her moving schools so I could take my rightful spot as the star. Yes, occasionally I had a twinge of envy so I certainly wasn't perfect, but I was really conscious not to let it get in the way of our friendship. Lucky I kept a lid on it because we became really good friends. We danced, hung out and shared roles together, two peas in a pod. We were the top two dancers in our class, but I knew there was a pretty sizeable gap between her and me, which I adjusted to because it was obvious that Rachel was extra special.

As I watched Rachel rise, it felt easier to be happy for her and it was obvious that she deserved all of her success. I also realised that what she had was far out of my reach. She worked hard and eventually became a soloist at The Royal Ballet in London, then a principal dancer at The Australian Ballet. I saw her dance a few times with The Australian Ballet and she was glorious, a true artist with mesmerising talent and a lovely soul. Even though I didn't get to live my dream, I'm so glad she was able to live hers. She deserved it.

◆

The bit of nonsense I couldn't avoid during that time, however, was the constant chatter about the race to be the thinnest. Being the thinnest in the class was good, it was desired, it was the pinnacle. I wanted to wear this crown, but I really, really liked food. I don't remember Rachel being concerned about her body, but there was a big group who were. We were quite certain about what we believed to be the perfect ballet body, and we were learning from each other that the shape of our bodies could make or break our careers. There was incessant whispers about the body shapes of our peers whose body parts we craved. 'So and so has no bum', 'so and so has tiny thighs' and on and on it went.

We would read *Dolly* magazines and pore over photos of the perfect girls, study diets and share ways to lose weight, because we felt that puberty and curves were something to fight. Today we are beginning to see a diverse range of body shapes on billboards outside shops and in advertising, but back then, not so much; it was an onslaught of skinny women adorning the pages of the magazines that we devoured. I was lucky not to grow up in the era of Instagram, though, because that stuff is next-level and I'm not sure how it would have affected me.

I listened to tips and tricks from my friends about how to make myself leaner to elevate my balletic physique and to my horror someone suggested that I stop eating my nightly treat of Milo and ice cream. Do you know how good Milo and ice cream is? That was never going to happen, so I searched for another way. A friend suggested that I should vomit after my meals like she did, and though I tried and tried, I just couldn't make myself throw up. Skipping meals seemed like the last resort so I attempted to discard my lunch every day. The problem was by the time I got home I was so starving I would end up consuming twice the food I would have if I had just eaten lunch. Nothing worked. I was useless at this.

I really love food and I love to cook. Plus I have an inclination toward hangriness so none of these twisted ballet diets really worked for me mentally, let alone physically. I was brought up around people who showed their love for others through cooking and I have always liked to do the same. So I had this weird dichotomy swirling around in my head. Food was the thing that made me happy, but I was starting to feel guilty about enjoying it. As hard as I tried to resist it, the lure of food was too great; I was dancing about twelve hours a week so I had good reason to be hungry. But as my love of food continued, the love for my body was waning.

Being so consumed by what our bodies look like can lead us to forget to appreciate all the amazing things they can do. The idea that if I wasn't aesthetically perfect then I was broken was a lie I fell for in my youth, and I feel cheated that I did. I was striving to succeed in an environment that was consumed by the idea of physical perfection, and I had no idea that years later I was going to enter an industry that had a similar focus. For now, though, I was like most teenage girls and I was coming to the realisation that your appearance could determine not just how you saw yourself, but how others related to you. It's a pity I can't say that the world proved me wrong; in fact, life consistently helped to ram that point home.

CHAPTER EIGHT

Honesty and kindness enhance every beauty.

SICILIAN PROVERB

It will be so much fun being the new kid at school in Year 9, said no teenager ever. Anyway, that's what happened: we left Canberra and back to Melbourne we went. I was a bit too old to pull off an American accent and a ballet headband so I walked into the lion's den with a half grown-out perm and the wrong shoes. Everyone was wearing brown T-bar sandals and I had yellow 'banana' shoes. They were basically a bird poo yellow chunky shoe with a big seam down the front and they were ugly as hell. I have tried to google them, but even the internet seems to have deleted them from history – that's how bad they were. Mum had tried to warn me off buying them, but they were all the rage in Canberra and I thought they could make the transition to Sacre Coeur, a fairly fancy all-girls Catholic school in Glen Iris. They could not. They were instantly a talking point and to this day my friends still mention them just to keep me grounded. I recently caught them telling my daughter about this fashion indiscretion as I screamed at them, 'Dear God, when will this end?!' I have to accept that the banana shoe trauma of 1987 will never leave me.

I had a rocky start at Sacre Coeur, but after about a year I eventually found great friends (and more acceptable footwear). There are of course pros and cons of moving schools a lot: the pros are that it can make you socially adaptable, and that would help me many times as I grew older (hello, *Survivor*). The cons are that in the fight to survive you learn to fit in at any cost and sometimes it is hard to work out who you are because your authentic self tends to be 'whatever makes me popular'. In Year 9 I found myself trying to climb to the top of the social ladder in my new school because I had learnt that the safest place in school is standing behind people at the top. (Hello *Survivor* again.)

The truly great thing about our move back to Melbourne was that I was finally reunited with my grandparents, who I had missed terribly. The years that followed with them were unforgettable. I was so lucky to have them. Leaving my friends in Canberra was sad, but Katherine and I stayed friends and we've managed to call each other on our birthday every year since then – we have never missed one.

◆

Even though I had to leave the Dell Brady School when we moved, ballet remained my passion. The good thing was Nicole was dancing at the same school as me so I never felt alone. It was nice having her around because she wasn't at high school with me anymore, which made me a bit sad as I missed having my older sister around. Nicole was a great dancer, but she didn't have the same love for it that I did. She was naturally talented and had cooler leotards than me, which I incessantly stole, but she wasn't obsessed. We both started together at a new ballet school in Melbourne that had a reputation for grooming young dancers to be suitable candidates for The Australian Ballet School, which was ultimately where I wanted to be. My dream was still very clear.

The ballet school was in the inner city. A lot of our time was spent hanging about, snacking and gossiping before class. I really felt like I was somewhere important. We were expected to be groomed and professional and our precise, tight buns were seen as an expression of our commitment – these expectations made me feel special. Coming from Canberra, it felt exciting to be in a big city studying ballet, catching the tram and seeing all of the hustle and bustle on the street.

Our school was run by a very passionate woman who I idolised because she was strict, elegant and so attractive; her approval meant everything to me. I had taken some classes with the same woman when I was young, and she seemed to have taken a shine to me so I was looking forward to working with her. I'd lost a little confidence after being in Canberra, I think purely by being outshone by someone more talented, so I was intent on starting fresh and working hard. And I did. The nights were cold and the work was tough, but I was fiercely determined. I was surrounded by incredible dancers. A few even went on to succeed at The Australian Ballet so I knew that I was in the right place.

Over the years I had met some inspiring teachers, mostly elite guest instructors like Margot Fonteyn and Ann Jenner, who were passionate about dance and loved to encourage the new generation, and I always hung on their every word and relished their praise. My new teacher wasn't quite as accomplished as those women, but she was respected and charismatic. Plus she was driven in a way that inspired me. I looked up to her as a guide and a confidante and we began what I viewed as a special mentor/prodigy relationship. Our dealings were intimate and intense and I felt like I had finally found my place in the world. I completely loved her. There were several of us who she took under her wing, and I felt an intense privilege to be one of the chosen few. I know now that children who are very driven are exceptionally vulnerable and it just takes one bad seed to ruin their potential and crush their dreams. Unfortunately for me, this teacher was that seed.

◆

I'm not sure what changed with my teacher, but when it happened, it felt swift and brutal. For starters, I think embarking on early teenagehood meant that I was tired a lot. I'm sure I wasn't as vibrant as I could have been, but I was growing and I could get a bit worn out. I was still working exceptionally hard, but occasionally when I was on the barre I wouldn't push myself. Like most warm-ups, the barre was always a bit boring to me and I felt like things really didn't become enjoyable until you hit the floor.

Previously my teacher had been supportive and affectionate in her interactions, but I started to notice small instances of cruelty, sly comments about my body, and then, slowly, she began to ice me out. It was like that awful feeling when a friend turns on you and you wrack your brain trying to think of what you have done wrong. It wasn't unusual for me to feel the wrath of her fingernails digging into my skin or squeezing my flesh as I worked, but the torment became longer, harder and more personal each week.

The teacher began to hover near me incessantly at barre time and any wrong move I made would result in those long fingernails ramming into me or her hand smacking me hard on the butt while she quietly delivered messages of disgust in my ear.

I refused to resign myself to this fate so I worked harder to try to win her back and just when it felt hopeless, she would lavish me with enough love and praise so that we reset and I could unwittingly head down the path to destruction all over again. I guess that's a cycle of abuse? Is it? I still don't know. What I'm sure of is that it wasn't good – it was destructive. I remember sitting on the stairs before class one day feeling nervous because she was in a bad mood – I could tell it was going to be a tough lesson. I remember my friend looking at me and saying, 'She only hurts those of us she really believes in, it means we're good dancers, so you only really need to worry if it stops.' Ballet schools are gossipy places so I wasn't sure if that was true, but it gave me comfort. I started to misinterpret her aggression as an act of love.

As it dragged on I became less and less like my usually perky self. I was still trying to fit in at school and this ballet experience was leaving me riddled with anxiety, although I didn't interpret it as such. My ballet days were filled with peaks and troughs: one day I was the golden child, the next I would be yelled at for stopping class as my toes bled. I was told that if I wasn't bleeding through to the outside of my shoes then I had no right to rest! (The fabric on ballet shoes is very thick, just quietly.)

Mum continued checking in with me at the time. I guess she could sense something was up, but I would tell her

I was fine because I thought that I was. My sister wasn't particularly enjoying the ballet school, but she says that she had a less visible spot in the pecking order, so she escaped the worst of it. And we were in different classes, so she never really saw what I was going through.

As time went on, my brain was being manipulated by a confusing mix of approval and insult, my weight fluctuated due to the fact that I have always had what the Italians would describe as 'a nervous stomach'. My body was bearing the brunt of my stress and I noticed that when I was jumping or lifting my legs it felt like I was moving through mud. My arms were heavy, my brain was foggy and the natural spring that I'd always possessed seemed to be gone. I'm assuming now that it was a physical reaction to mental distress, but at the time I just thought there was something wrong with my body. I tried to push through and hide it because it felt shameful and scary.

Then a sliding doors moment occurred in which my life drastically altered course.

I was in class holding onto the barre, with my right leg lifting up and down in one of our regular warm-up exercises. The teacher was standing in front, yelling instructions. She was grumpy, that was clear, and I was being called on a lot. My teacher had piercing eyes and I could see her staring at me as I was lifting my leg higher, but I just couldn't seem to please her, my leg felt so heavy.

I knew something was coming for me, but I wasn't sure what until my name was screamed out in a tone that was filled with vile rage. I was beckoned to stand at the front of the class and everyone was told to stop what they were doing and look at me.

'Look at her!' she screamed and pointed out my laziness. Then, just to nail her point home, she yelled, 'Everyone look at her legs, because if you slack off and don't work hard, you are going to end up with fat legs like Pia.' Everyone stared at me; no-one enjoyed it, although I could sense the relief in the room that they had escaped her wrath.

'Now continue,' she told the class. I went to return to the barre, but she grabbed me hard and told me to stay. 'You do your exercises here so the class can look at you and your fat legs as a reminder of what can happen if you are lazy. Now lift!'

As I lifted my leg she would angrily yell, 'Fat, fat, fat.' So I stayed in my spotlight of shame and I finished my exercises while she reminded the class to keep looking at me.

I went home and carried the trauma with me silently until it was time to go to ballet again, but I couldn't do it. My mum loved ballet, really loved it, so I was perhaps keeping it a secret from her from a misguided fear of being a disappointment. I'd never refused to go to ballet before and when I finally told her what had happened, I saw her face change.

The next thing I knew she was on the phone. I could hear her screaming down the line, all upper-case outrage (Mum didn't use profanities) and lots of 'HOW DARE YOU' and 'NO, YOU LISTEN TO ME!' I felt a sense of relief and confusion because the person I was so scared of was on the other end of the line, being ripped a new arsehole by my mother. It felt good, but I was also struggling with the loss of my mentor. I remember thinking, 'Wow I didn't know mums could do that!'

'You never have to go back there,' Mum said after she finished the call. And I never did.

◆

I moved to The National Theatre Ballet school, which was another prestige school that suited me better for many reasons. I reconnected with some great teachers and found it to be a healthier environment for a young dancer to push themselves in. I tried hard, I really did, but I couldn't seem to lift myself out of the swamp I was in. The more time went on, the heavier my body got. My legs were heavy, my arms were heavy and I couldn't find the passion and excitement for ballet that I once held. Some days I would make a pact with myself to dance at my absolute peak in class and the teachers would always notice and encourage me to keep pushing, but eventually the muddy feeling would return and my body would become heavy again. I used to bounce around effortlessly, feeling light as a feather with joy in my face whenever I danced, but all that seemed to have faded away.

Was I burnt-out or had I been hurt too badly? I don't know the answer. It was probably a mix of both. The fight for lightness was so hard and I tried to find it, I really did, but in my final year of school I decided to take a break from ballet to concentrate on my studies. I kept thinking, 'One day I will go back', but I just couldn't find the courage.

◆

It's not fair to blame my failure or the death of my ambition on one person, I know that, but sometimes I do wonder what could have been. Maybe it would have ended up the same and I'm focusing outward rather than looking inward? The truth is, I don't know for sure. Whatever it was, I can see how lucky I am to have found another road for my creative expression. Aside from ballet, films and books were my passion, so that's where I decided to direct my energy, and I am grateful I was able to pursue those dreams.

I don't know if I would have told this story or even registered how I felt if it hadn't been for a chance encounter at a fashion parade in the early 2000s. I was sitting in the front row waiting for the show to start and a gentleman sitting behind me tapped my shoulder. 'Pia,' he said and introduced himself. He explained that he worked in the media and often saw me at events, so his wife had asked him to pose a question to me if we ever met. 'My wife went to the same ballet school as you in Melbourne and she always wanted to ask if you are okay . . . because she isn't.'

I felt like I had been hit by a truck, but I laughed nervously and shrugged it off. 'Oh, yeah, it was awful, hahaha . . . tell her I said hi . . . hahaha.' The parade started and I found myself sitting in the dark feeling disturbed because I knew something meaningful had happened; I just didn't know what. I hadn't really discussed it over the years, except for trotting out the 'fat, fat, fat' story occasionally after a few drinks to shock people at parties. I had pushed it down and locked it away until that moment. I spent the whole parade barely registering the pretty dresses in front of me as the feelings I had ignored slowly made themselves known. When the parade ended I quickly sought out the man, grabbed him by the arm and said, 'Please tell her I'm actually not sure if I'm okay, but let her know that she isn't alone . . . and say thanks.'

CHAPTER NINE

As long as you live, you always learn.

ITALIAN SAYING

I thought giving up ballet would be harder than it was. Turns out being a teenager with no commitments is actually pretty fantastic. Everyone tells you 'it's the best time of your life' and it was, but it's hard to fully embrace every opportunity because there are the frustrations that go along with it. Not enough money, not enough freedom and a lack of appreciation of the collagen that is plumping up your dewy skin. However, if the teen years go right, it can set you up for the rest of your life. This all depends on the company you keep and this was one part of my life that I nailed, because the people I surrounded myself with were golden. I had a great bunch of girlfriends at high school and my friends outside of school really set the standard for healthy male friendships for the years to come.

It was difficult to give up all of the physical activity that had been such a big part of my life for so many years; luckily soon after I finished ballet mum signed us up to a seven-week yoga course. I found my new home. Yoga made me happier, it made me kinder and it kept me feeling strong. I liked the philosophy, I loved the smell of incense burning in the room (still do) and I knew it was the key for keeping me balanced. My commitment would come and go over the years, but it was always there in the background, waiting patiently for me.

School itself was okay, but there was a lot of academic pressure and I had the impression that most of the teachers found me annoying. I seemed to please my art and drama teachers, but I could tell that sometimes I irked the rest. I've always joked that I'm like an anchovy: if you are into me you want me on everything, but if you aren't a fan the negative reaction will be quite potent. People always laugh a bit too hard when I tell them this analogy, so it must ring true. I really love anchovies, so I'm okay with it I guess.

Sacre Coeur was located in a beautiful old Gothic-style building surrounded by a magnificent garden estate. It has had some additions more recently, but the exquisite castle still sits on top of the hill and looms above those who pass by below. The chapel was old and ornate, and attached to the school was the nuns' convent which housed the sisters who would come and socialise with us occasionally. One of them was exceptionally spirited – she used to talk incessantly about romance and regale us with tales of her forbidden love life with priests.

For the most part the nuns I've met in my life have been pretty great people, filled with an enthusiasm for life and varying degrees of commitment to the constraints of the sisterhood.

I was too chatty, too silly and too headstrong for a strict Catholic girls school that demanded academic perfection. Saying that, I appreciated the direction I received there because without it, I'm not sure I would have gone to university and I am grateful that I did.

English and history were subjects that I excelled in, so I leant on them to raise my grades; the rest of my classes I found a bit boring, but that's not unusual for a teenager. The teachers were a patchy bunch. Most of them were fairly patient considering they had to deal with a lot of hormones and a bit of cheek. Even though it wasn't perfect, for a strict Catholic girls school in the 1980s, it wasn't bad.

Once I survived my tricky first year of being the new kid, I ended up having a vibrant and fun time. The friendships I made were deep, strong and have lasted a lifetime. I even managed to save one new student, Diana, from the depths of oblivion when she turned up in Year 11 with her perm growing out and suspiciously familiar European features. I like to think of it as my hero moment (something I tend to remind her of just to keep her loyal). It turned out that Diana was Croatian, and I knew we ethnic girls with misguided perm choices needed to stick together. I introduced myself in maths class and promised to look after her because 'I was growing my body wave out when I started here too and it was hell'. Luckily, she was smart enough to wear the right shoes.

I took Diana under my wing until her hair was long enough for the perm to be cut out and she could fly free. She stuck with me though, and once we left school we ended up as flatmates for years, which wasn't always smooth sailing due to my obsessive need for order and neatness, and her penchant for leaving the weekend newspaper strewn all over the lounge room floor.

The friendships I made at Sacre Coeur (after my awkward banana shoes year) were amazing, and I'm happy to say my school friends are still my best friends to this day. There are six of us who have stayed more than friends – we feel like family. We've travelled, fought, laughed and cried together for over thirty years. We have held each other's hands through all the ups and downs, all our mistakes and triumphs. We all turn fifty very soon and even though some things about getting older are a bit sucky, I am thankful we are all here because some of us did a lot of silly stuff in our twenties (not all of us, but I'm definitely one of the guilty ones). Anyway, it's a blessing that we get to grow old together and I'm forever thankful for those women.

◆

Being back in Melbourne meant I got to spend some very precious time with my grandparents. I wasn't *too* rebellious as a teenager (I saved that for my early twenties) and I think part of the reason for that was because of the time I spent with them. Most days after school I would walk over to my nan's house and have lemon slice or chocolate hedgehog and sit in front of the gas heater drinking tea while her little sausage dog, Herbie, kept me company. When I was sick or had to study hard, I would pack my bags and move in to be looked after in that comforting way that only grandparents can offer, just because I loved being there. Nanna's cookie jar was always filled with chocolate chip biscuits, and her fridge stocked with Neapolitan ice cream and a fresh jug of green cordial ready to guzzle on a hot day. In winter her lamb shank soup and pot roasts were a staple and there was always a cup of hot Milo before bed.

Luckily I had quickly committed to eating over starving myself because my nonna was never going to stop feeding me. When I went to Nonna's, the delicious food she made was an endless production line of incredible rustic Italian meals that would soothe your soul from the inside out.

Everything was rich yet simple and her apartment would always smell like there was something mouth-watering on the stove, because there always was. If you can conjure up a clichéd idea of what an Italian nonna's house would smell like, it was exactly that. Sometimes in high school I would tell Nonna I was coming for dinner and I would surprise her with three extra friends – there were still plates of leftovers for us all to take home. Everyone loved her. I could tell that she was lonely sometimes, she loved having people over and it was always her food that helped to make them stay. I sometimes wonder if I did enough to help alleviate her loneliness, or let her know just how much I loved her. Every old picture I have of her I'm hanging off her arm like I never wanted to let her go, so I'm sure she knew, but at this point I was a teenager and I mostly thought of myself. It's hard to remember to do those things in the moment because it all goes fast. Nonna was a constant in my life and I thought she would always be around.

I learnt to cook by hanging out in Nonna's kitchen, simply by helping out. I realised years later that I had been taught all of these recipes without any formal instruction simply by the two of us spending time together. That's the beautiful thing about tradition, sometimes it's a slow burn. I should have asked more questions (especially about the *zuppa di fagioli*) but back then I didn't realise how special our time together was. I just thought of her as my nonna who would be by my side forever, but the brave, strong Angelina had lived through so much upheaval and had so much to teach.

◆

Movement was still important to me in my final years of high school and along with my new-found love for yoga, I also found a passion for aerobics. Yes, aerobics (I know), so I threw myself into that to keep my mind and body as healthy as possible. I decided that I would try to become an aerobics instructor, so I did work experience at a gym and even gave aerobics classes at school, which sounds like social suicide, but somehow didn't end in trauma for either me or my aerobics students (aka classmates).

Aerobics gave me a gift. There was an aged-care facility down the street from my grandparents' house, so I decided to volunteer to give aerobics lessons to the residents, which I thought would be impressive on my CV. I had no formal qualifications and I didn't even have first-aid training, but everyone thought it was a great idea. What could go wrong? These were the days before workplace safety and public liability insurance were a thing, so in I trotted with a pair of Reeboks on my feet and a head full of dreams ready to take on the world, or in this case, an aged-care home in Malvern.

Most of the residents stayed in their chairs for the classes, so I decided that we would use walking canes instead of barbells, which really took things to the next level. What a time we had grooving to the beat of Technotronic and sharing a laugh. I am eternally thankful to God that no-one broke a hip.

Afterwards, when we had worked up a very mild sweat, we would share some tea and biscuits – my passion for a biscuit reward never waned. In hindsight the fact that a teenage girl with no qualifications was permitted to give aerobics classes to elderly citizens was probably dangerous, but it was also fairly comedic. We all had harmless fun and it helped me realise two of my lifelong passions, a cuppa and old people.

◆

I managed my last year of high school in a pretty happy place and although I continued to struggle with letting go of my ballet body, I found that without the scrutiny those classes brought on I could release that valve of pressure and stress and let loose. I still felt a pang of shame if my jeans got tight, but I forced myself to push through because those mental gymnastics were exhausting. I felt free. Part of the fun of that time was eating pizza, drinking beer and hanging out with friends and I managed to keep the demons at bay enough to be able to truly enjoy myself in the moment.

The final year of school is such a complicated time. There is so much pressure and there is also the exciting carrot at the end of the stick because the finish line is so close. I liked to study hard, but I also dove headfirst into having lots of fun; after years of discipline and structure, I was letting loose.

My neighbourhood was a very social place and I lived close to school. I had my girlfriends, but I also hung out with a great mix of local boys who lived in my suburb and they became my weekend buddies. So if I wasn't at Nonna's or Nanna's I was hanging out at someone's house in the afternoons, chilling and watching TV. They were good times, really good.

My after-school walk took me through Central Park, which is a picturesque park surrounded by gorgeous leafy maple trees and roaming pathways. Even though it was a charming aesthetic we were never keen to hang out there for too long and my walks home turned into a quick jog as I cut through the trees before getting to the safety of the street.

The thing about the 1980s was that there was no internet, meaning that perverts needed to leave the comfort of their homes to get their kicks, so they hung around in parks. Parks near Catholic girls high schools, to be exact. To say I saw more than my fair share of erect penises lurking in the bushes on my travels home would be a massive understatement. I'm surprised I was ever receptive to one in my adult life because in my teenage years they were always presented unsolicited and were very unappealing. Putting aside the appalling behaviour of these abrupt indecencies, the creativity of some of these criminals intrigued me. They came from all angles and in different costumes: a towel on the head (weird), an overcoat (cliché), a balaclava (terrifying). Once a man sitting in his car asked my friend and me for directions and when we peered inside, we saw he had his large erection placed neatly on top of the Melways in order to sell his story. I was impressed by his use of the map as a prop and commitment to character, but by this stage we were desensitised to such indecent assaults and didn't even scream.

I didn't really think about the impact of these encounters until years later, when I was at drama school in New York. A friend came running into the classroom crying and panicking because she said a man had masturbated outside the phone box she was standing in. When she stopped talking I said, 'Yeah, but what else happened, why are you crying?' Her look of horror said it all and the penny dropped. All those penises I saw on my walks home were a really bad thing and I had just been programmed into a state of acceptance. Sometimes I mention it to women my age and they say, 'Oh my God, the penises! They were everywhere. I forgot!'

◆

Uninvited penises aside, I truly believe that something magical happened in those years that grounded me and gave me some deep sense of self and belonging.

My parents loved having a busy house and my dad played the part of the cheerful eighties Italian caricature to perfection. He loved to put on a spread and share a drink with everyone and he made sure the bar and fridge were always stocked. He decorated himself with lots of gold jewellery and he was a larger-than-life character, which my friends found welcoming. Our door was never locked so you could walk in anytime and make yourself at home.

My mum was into baking bread and she would always have something in the oven ready to go – hot cinnamon scrolls were a fan favourite. There was a slight hiccup during one sleepover when a friend who was drunk lost his way to the toilet and urinated on her industrial-sized bag of flour in the walk-in pantry, but she eventually got over it.

Nicole was in her twenties and still living at home and she would lend me her ID so I could get into nightclubs and, even though at seventeen I still looked twelve, somehow I got away with it. My size could be a disadvantage. One night out, while mixing $2 tap beers with lime cordial, I didn't know my limit. I was small and it hit me hard. I started vomiting up green sludge. My friend Marcus's mum picked me up and snuck me into my house so my parents wouldn't know.

'Sleep on your side,' she instructed, 'do not roll on your back and choke!' I lay on my side all night, not sure what she meant, but too scared to move or sleep. We were lucky to have that kind of big family vibe in my neighbourhood where our friends' parents would be looking out for us and be there when we made mistakes along the way.

I thought I was set for life living in East Malvern and I never wanted to leave. I had my girlfriends from school close by and we were such a tight-knit group. Then my gang of East Malvern buddies just made my teenage years and early twenties wonderful. We had endless amounts of fun, house hopping and hanging out. I imagined growing old in the same suburb as them all and eventually having kids who would all be friends like we were; everything would be amazing and idyllic.

Unfortunately, life doesn't work that way and even though things fell apart, I realise now that all was not lost. Without those people and that wonderful experience of joyous friendship, I wouldn't be who I am. I know how lucky I was to have those glory years. My school friends are still very much a part of my life and although I don't see my gang of neighbourhood mates often anymore, I still love them . . . always will.

PART TWO

PART TWO

CHAPTER TEN

The vase filled with water sooner
or later will break or crash.

SICILIAN PROVERB

Although school ending and your teen years turning into twenties can be a bit sad, I threw myself into university life in a big way. I loved studying. Cinema studies and drama were my favourite classes of my Bachelor of Arts degree. I loved walking around campus pretending I was at Oxford, keeping an eye out for cute guys in my RM Williams boots, high waisted jeans and Sportsgirl bodysuit. (Finally, that sounds like a cute outfit!) Thursday nights out were always fun as Fridays were free of classes. Saturdays were reserved for working in retail and Sundays were all about lazy days with friends. I'd kept the same friends through my teenage years and we seemed to find a nice balance between studying, working and hitting The Armadale Hotel, a staple in our social life. That pub is a Woolworths these days, and I always feel a pang of nostalgia whenever I walk past.

I wasn't dwelling on my bad premonitions as much as I used to and I was content most of the time. There wasn't that much to fear – even then I knew those were some of the best days of my life.

You know those moments you end up forever regretting? The ones you would give anything to go back and do differently? I've had a few, but there's one from this time in my life that stands out. Nonna had called. She was up for a chat. She wasn't usually chatty on the phone but on this particular evening she was. I was heading out with friends and I was eager to get out the door, so I kept trying to wind up the conversation. Eventually I said abruptly, 'Nonna, I have to go!' I didn't think much of it because I'd arranged to see her the next week. I could tell she was feeling a bit lonely, but I spoke to her most days. There was always tomorrow.

The next morning I sat on the couch watching TV, thinking how I would do anything to get out of work or avoid my university assignment that was due. I was tired and I just couldn't be bothered with anything. I think I was still half-asleep when I saw Dad answering the phone. He listened and then put his hand on the kitchen bench. His head slumped over. I thought he was about to pass out. By that stage, he was a bit round and red in the face so he often looked to me like he was on the verge of a heart attack. I was used to watching him closely.

Dad stayed in that position for a minute. Then he straightened up, returned to the call, said thank you and walked off down the hall in a way I had never seen him move before. I wasn't too panicked, but I did stare down the hallway waiting to hear what had happened. Eventually Dad came back, stood in front of me and said, 'Nonna just died, in church . . . Nonna died.'

It felt like my world ended.

Nope, no, no no no. Nope. No. I wasn't ready for this, I didn't want it and I still don't. I couldn't help thinking of our shitty last phone call and about how this must have been my fault. Why do we always think death must be our fault or that we have done something bad or wrong to hurt the person who died? The years of love between us were obliterated in my mind and all I was left with was that last conversation in which I was a shithead.

Most of us have lost someone we love. If you are lucky it doesn't happen until you are older, but once you have experienced it, you know how deep the pain can go. Losing Nonna made the world around me feel suddenly different, the ground wasn't so solid. It hurt so much. It still does.

A great life deserves a good death and the only sweet part of this story is that Nonna definitely got that. Just before she died she told me that she kept dreaming about her dead sisters standing on the steps of St Anthony's Church, calling her to come in. I didn't think much of this because we were a highly superstitious family and were always sharing our strange dreams. I guess her sisters knew she was coming back to them. On the day she died, Nonna left some soup bubbling away on the stove to have for lunch later that day, then left home and walked to church to attend Sunday morning mass. She sat in a pew next to a nice gentleman who later called and kindly told us every moment until her last breath. They shook hands and said, 'Peace be with you' to each other. Right near the end of the service, Nonna flopped her head on his shoulder, which seemed odd to this man because he didn't know her, but he didn't push her away. Then he noticed she was gone. Church was halted, there was a big commotion as people tried to save Angelina, but God had taken her home. That was the end of her story. But not the end of her impact, especially on me.

Nonna liked a fuss, she liked attention and she loved church, so I figure this was the perfect send-off. I just wish it was my shoulder she'd rested her head on; I would have liked to say goodbye. They said her heart stopped because it was enlarged from her diabetes and it just gave out. I thought it was poignant that she died from an enlarged heart because she had the biggest heart of anyone I had ever met.

Italians really go all out when it comes to death and funerals; we wear black and we mourn for a long time. The night before a funeral we all come together to pray the rosary and have a viewing of the body, where it is customary to kiss the cheek of the deceased as a symbol of respect. I couldn't manage that for Nonna. I knew she would have looked perfect, but it was too hard for me. I didn't want to say goodbye and I didn't want that memory of her lying dead. Nonna was never still. My sister couldn't do it either, we are similarly anxious when it came to death. The wailing I liked though, it tapped into how I felt like everyone knew the world was a worse place without my nonna and that she would never be forgotten.

The wailing continued the next day at the funeral, when Nonna's sister screamed and fell to the ground and threatened to throw herself into the coffin. I felt pleased. I liked the drama and I liked that someone was giving a publicly theatrical rendition of the turmoil that was sickening my soul. The grey sky also played along by adding to the drama and there was a slow drizzle dampening the day, which seemed cinematic and poetic.

After the church service, I waited at the gravesite for the line of mourners to give their condolences. I remember looking down the hill and seeing a long line of chocolate-brown-haired people wearing black that stretched as far as I could see. So much love was sent our way that day from family and people who I barely knew. This is the beauty of Italian tradition because the memory of that outpouring of love got me through whenever I felt over-whelmingly sad. It made me proud of who Italians are as people and I started to make sense of all that talk about death and funeral shrouds and removing curses. My nonna and zias weren't misguided; they just knew that death and sadness are inevitable and so they were trying to make sense of it in their own way while alive.

After Nonna's death, things became a bit messy, as they tend to do when death, money and Sicilians are involved. It was the end of an era. The emotion of coming to terms with that loss saw some blow-ups and drama – I wonder if everyone wanted a piece of her or if they wanted more? Luckily my dad managed to get me a couple of things that she had always promised me. A gold brooch in the shape of an A, because my middle name was her name, and a funny piece of costume jewellery I loved that I used to put in my mouth because it looked like a set of teeth. The one thing I really wanted was the red-and-white servi-ette with my nonno's old life in it: the coins, the licence and the half-empty packet of Camel cigarettes. My heart hurt in desperation and I kept asking for it, not willing to tell everyone why it meant so much to me. I could tell from my dad's face he wanted me to stop asking and I assumed that someone had taken it or maybe they had unknowingly thrown it in the trash. I couldn't believe it was gone and I couldn't believe she was gone and subsequently most of my Italian family was gone too. In classic Sicilian tradition they were quickly forgotten and never spoken of again, so I didn't mourn for them, not one bit. But I never stopped mourning for Nonna. I wore that gold brooch next to my heart for the longest time so I could feel her close to me. Angelina's story was over, but her story became part of my story and then by telling it, I feel like I have kept her alive . . . just a little bit.

CHAPTER ELEVEN

The world is made of stairs,
some go down, and some go up.

ITALIAN SAYING

Life and time moves on, as it always does, but somehow Nonna's soul leaving the earth felt like the beginning of my adult life starting; real life with all of its ups and downs, traumas and unsettling experiences. Even so, I knew that I was lucky and for the most part I was happy. Work stress, money worries and heartbreak were all coming for me. The world as I knew it was slowly changing.

Sometimes I teach young drama students who are full of talent and ambition and all the hopefulness that comes with being at the beginning of their career. A number of them often feel frustrated at their inability to find raw emotion and access the deep pain that can be needed for a great performance, because they are young and still full of hope.

That is a good thing for life, but understanding pain and the human condition is the actor's best tool. I always remind young actors that just by living life, emotional knowledge will come, because I'm pretty sure no-one gets to escape pain. Every heartbreak, tragedy and failure can be packed away in the actor's section of the brain to use when needed; at least then it can serve a positive purpose.

One of my first jobs in my post–high school life was in an Indian restaurant in Malvern called Mem Sahibs, where a school friend of mine worked as well. It was your classic hole-in-the-wall joint with vinyl tables and old-school charm. Cyril who ran the restaurant was awesome and took us under his wing in the loveliest way. I always thought he was really old, but in hindsight he was probably in his early forties, maybe even his thirties. He was the best first boss you could ask for. The food was incredible and sometimes people would line the streets to get a meal; other nights would be dead so we would sit around drinking lassis and talk.

Cyril would never clean his pan between one dish and the next, which sounds like a bad thing, but was anything but because the food would get richer and more complex as the night went on. With each new order he would keep adding more flavour to the old sauce and it turned into such a magically intense curry, which would eventually become our dinner at the end of our shift. To this day I have never eaten curry as delicious as Cyril's; plus I also learnt a few handy waitressing tips while working there. For example, if you clear wine bottles from the table with just a small amount of wine left in them, the patrons don't notice and then you can mix all of the dregs together, which means we would all get a glass of wine with our end-of-shift meal. I would expertly plan the moment when I would whip the wine away and if I ever got caught I'd smile sweetly and say, 'Oh, so sorry, I had no idea there was any left.' We never mixed red with white, because we weren't animals, but it wasn't unusual to have a nice sav blanc/chardonnay/riesling mix at the end of the evening. Honestly, it's not as bad as it sounds.

I worked at Mem Sahibs for around three years and even after I left I would pop in to see Cyril for a curry and a chat. He was more than a boss, he felt like family. He visited me in hospital when I had glandular fever, he rescued me when my car broke down and he was always there to talk about life and teach me about India and its food. The restaurant shut down eventually and we lost touch, but I think about him often. After years of working in pubs and nightclubs with sleazy and boozy bosses, Cyril's light burns even brighter in my mind. How lucky I was to know him and work for him. I can still make a mean samosa in record time thanks to Cyril and although I don't mix my wine anymore, I'm not totally opposed to the idea.

◆

Around this time, as I was powering through university, life was starting to speed up, as it does when you get older. The actor Marshall Napier once told me that we interpret time in relation to how long we have been alive, so when we are two, a year is half of our life, but when we are sixty, a year is a sixtieth of our life so it seems quite short. I think about this all the time because the older I become, the quicker Christmas rolls around.

Nanna and Grandfather were still a huge part of my life in my early twenties, although Grandfather's health was going downhill, which was hard to witness. When he eventually passed away, it was different to Nonna's death because we didn't want him to suffer anymore. His last years were confused and difficult for him – when he left us it felt like it was the right time. He used to work on the security desk at the ABC, so now whenever I walk in there I always give an especially friendly greeting to whoever is behind the desk because it makes me think of him.

It's the reality for everyone that eventually life stops and we have to say goodbye; unfortunately we can't control when that happens.

But it wasn't all loss in those years. My East Malvern gang of friends were still my favourite people to spend time with and boy, did we have a lot of fun, rolling from house to house with no responsibilities and not many worries. The worst stress we had was having enough money at the end of a night out to get a hotdog or possibly a kebab. I adored them all, but I was particularly close to Marcus – we became joined at the hip and I loved him deeply. I am bewitched by people who make me laugh and that's pretty much all we did. We would rent weird cartoons from Video Ezy or hang out in the afternoons watching Teenage Mutant Ninja Turtles and make popcorn or eat microwaved frozen hamburgers (don't judge me – it was a thing in the nineties.) Even though we were young adults, we were both still kids at heart.

We only ever had one fight. It was big, really big. He did something to upset me and I was mad. Really mad. I thought the only way to let him know how much he had hurt me was to ice him out. I blame too many mafia movies for some of my life choices.

He felt bad and told me so as he tried to apologise and make it right, but the blood of my nonno runs through my body, so I had to be sure he knew he'd betrayed me. I stopped talking to him for months, thinking that would teach him. But then the fire burnt out and I realised that I was missing Marcus and needed him back in my life. During it all I knew we would return to normal eventually. After many months we bumped into each other outside our favourite Video Ezy and my heart skipped a beat in a good way. We said hello to each other and smiled. At that moment we knew our fight was over, but I was off to the Gold Coast to work at Movie World for the summer, so it was left at that. I knew that when I returned home we would settle into something good again, maybe not the same friendship, but perhaps something better. We didn't get the chance though because he died that summer.

I was on the Gold Coast when I found out about the car accident. He was with our friends, who were also hurt. Life changed for so many people in that instant, as it does when tragedy strikes at random. I grieved for Marcus, for my amazing friends who I was scared wouldn't recover and for the shitty person I was to have punished him for not being perfect, for all of it. We never know what lies ahead, but I was too young to grasp that reality yet and not punish myself, so I just had to live with the regret.

Nothing was the same for any of us after Marcus died – his parents, his family, our friends. His short life left such an impact on so many. The weird thing is that when someone dies young, they grow old in your memories. At least that is the case for me. Whenever I think of Marcus, he is my age, still growing older in my head even though he stayed forever young on the earth.

I was so angry at myself for again having a bad final moment with someone I loved. Kiri, Nonna and then Marcus – when would I ever learn? It made me paranoid for years about saying goodbye to people; I had to make every goodbye perfect, just in case.

Eventually I placed Marcus in my Rolodex of pain that I would later tap into for my acting. I have different people and experiences in there and I'd flick through it each time I needed to cry or show hurt in a scene. Not every actor does this, but I find it's a way I can access truth. Paradoxically it's also a way for me to heal, to delve into those parts of my heart and exorcise the demons of agony.

CHAPTER TWELVE

Love doesn't listen to advice.

SICILIAN PROVERB

After years of avoiding serious romantic relationships like the plague, I was starting to warm to the idea of a boyfriend, but I just couldn't seem to meet anyone I liked enough. Was it me? Was I too much of a tomboy? Was I gay? Or were there no hot boys in Melbourne? The opposite sex seemed so underwhelming when it came to long-term romance. Boys appeared to like me and I liked them, but I couldn't find one that I wanted to make out with more than once or do more with than play Nintendo.

I've never been one for one-night stands because they don't agree with me, so I was happy just hanging with the boys my school friends and I knew, and watching surfing or snowboarding videos. I had some eclectic crushes: Tom Carroll (surfer), Mikhail Baryshnikov (dancer), David Bowie

(Ziggy Stardust era only), Luke Perry (I stand by this), but real live boys just didn't make the grade. Then Greg did.

He was one of a fun bunch of guys my friends and I often spent time with during our uni days. Greg and I hung out for months and became close friends. I liked his big blue eyes (tick), he made me laugh (tick) – and the ticks kept coming. First serious boyfriend box ticked, and lucky for me he was a good one.

Greg and I went out happily for a couple of years. We had so much fun and he was sweet to me, though he did do that young guy thing and sometimes get hammered, and I would have to drag him home in a cab . . . but that was the worst of it. He did manage to break my heart a little at the end, but he even did that well and we stayed friends. We still text and talk, and sometimes he sends me songs he thinks I'd like, which I do. Good ex-boyfriends definitely deserve a shoutout, so this is his.

◆

Halfway through my Arts degree I decided to switch it up, change university and become a performance art major. I did a lot of rolling around on the floor and grunting at my fellow students, but the best part was we got to write and create our own work. We would watch experimental plays, go and see bands and furiously study Pina Bausch, who became our hero. I liked it. I enjoy learning and the exploratory nature of it was exciting to me. We wrote and put on plays and I made friends who were wild and interesting.

After I moved on from waitressing I ended up working in nightclubs, which I liked because the work paid good money and was very social. Admittedly we spent way too much time ingesting things we shouldn't have and given these were the days when you could smoke indoors, I was grateful my lungs didn't give out. Mostly I sat on the door with another workmate asking people if they were on the guest list; if they weren't, they would have to pay an entry fee. Sounds pretty easy, but you did need a thick skin. I was the gatekeeper to fun, so drunken tirades came thick and fast.

It got particularly intense at a Boy George event when a guy knocked me to the ground and lay on top of me screaming, 'Fuck you bitch! I need to see him, but I'm not fucking paying!!!' Turns out people can be really passionate about Boy George, though it was only a $20 entry fee. Other times I was vomited on, strangled, slapped and spat at, but the friendly security boys would always step in, so it wasn't as scary as it sounds, and I earned good money and made some great friends while I was at it. Plus, when people were inebriated they often tipped very handsomely. Still, the work turned me off going to nightclubs for fun.

That nightclub chapter was followed by my snowboarding nightclub chapter. Yep, I really let those nun-loving ballet years eat my dust. I would work in clubs all year then escape to the snow for the winter holidays and work at bars in the ski fields. I spent three full seasons snowboarding and loving every minute of it, but I'd like to gloss over this period of time, if you don't mind, to avoid word getting back to my kids! But . . . you can imagine. Too much of everything and no vegetables. I'm surprised I eventually made it through university rather than following winters and working in bars for the rest of my life, which was somewhat tempting at the time. There is just one photo of me that my friend Jo has that might be incriminating, but I am pretty sure it's forever safe with her and, yes, I have my clothes on. Anyway, it's too funny to destroy.

◆

Around this time my sister had gotten married and started a family. A few years later, in true post-eighties style, my father's financial life fell apart at the same time as my parents' marriage. It was a bit on trend, as many of my friends' parents were suffering the same fate. Was it the excess of the eighties that brought them down? Who knows. Even though I was shocked by my family situation, I probably shouldn't have been. There was, however, a weird sort of shame that I carried around with me as the world I knew disintegrated. I don't think it's abnormal for children of divorce to feel envious of families that have kept it together, and I definitely felt that. I liked to go to friends' houses for family dinners and soak in all of that loveliness; it made me so happy, but also led me to lament what I had lost.

My own relationships were sometimes complicated at the time. Although working in clubs was fun, in hindsight the work probably didn't lend itself to presenting the best romantic opportunities for me. I also came to realise that, fun as working in bars and nightclubs was, there was a dark side to that world that was exhausting. I found myself with no real direction or goals, and for someone who had been so regimented and focused in my younger ballet days, it was unsettling.

I realise now how lost I was. There were many days when I couldn't imagine dragging myself out of the hole I had dug for myself and I feared that I never would. Looking back, I can see that I took away three major lessons from this time that I've been able to draw strength from ever since. Hopefully they might help someone else who feels like their life has run off track. Those lessons are:

- Never lose hope and always remember that you *do* deserve better.

- No matter how big the hole is, you can always dig yourself out if you retain a glimmer of belief in yourself; that tiny speck of light that still shines in your soul can save you.
- If the people around you are dragging you down, get rid of them, start fresh and know that there will always be people out there to forgive and support you. If there aren't many right away, don't despair – you will find them.

I knew my nonna would have been disappointed to see my spark diminished, so one morning I woke up and decided it was time to change everything. For good. I was determined to start my life afresh. So, one sunny day, my sister picked me up in her car and I went to live with her while I worked things out.

I bunked in a room on the floor with one of my nephews and as I snuggled up that first night under my Sesame Street doona cover listening to him snore, I felt whole for the first time in a long time. I could feel my life reset immediately. I loved being in Nicole's home among the hustle and bustle of a young family. She had two sons by this stage and I adored them. They were the cutest toddlers with dimples and Lego and dinosaur pyjamas and matchbox cars and fart jokes and an endless ability to make me laugh. I couldn't get enough of their squishy faces. (Still can't really, but they are grown men now so don't tell them.) Nothing will heal your soul quicker than spending your days lining up cars in perfect rows on the carpet or watching cartoons on repeat with a couple of cheeky boys. It was bliss and thanks to them, I was somewhat reborn.

CHAPTER THIRTEEN

The third time's the charm.

SICILIAN PROVERB

The preceding years had taken a toll, but I was certain I was on the up again. The good news is I earned my degree! The bad news is that I came to realise that people didn't care that much about a Bachelor of Arts, so no-one was knocking down my door to offer me work. The high school career adviser had not warned me about this. Even though the world didn't seem dazzled by my BA, I was still impressed with myself. It felt good.

I had moved into a place in Elwood with my friend Diana (the half-grown-out-perm friend from high school). We were great flatmates and quickly fell into a groove, despite my previously mentioned obsessive neatness. Well, there was the one time a seagull flew into our bathroom, got trapped inside and pooped on everything including our toothbrushes and towels. I was late for work that day so I left the mess and the bird to deal with later, secretly hoping she would deal with it all first. When I came home, the bathroom was sparkling and I feigned surprise. Bad flatmate award goes to . . . me. I worry that Diana has never really forgiven me, but apart from that hiccup, living together was a time of my life that I cherish.

Happily, I had finally scored an agent from a small agency thanks to my friend Jacinta Stapleton, who I had become close to after we met working at an advertising awards ceremony. We were paid to sit on stage in 1920s underwear and play cards. I distinctly remember she looked cute in her bustier and bloomers, but my underwear was too tight and squished my knees, which made them look like pickled people (eighties joke). The things we unemployed actors do for money can be pretty weird, and I never worked out why we needed to be in vintage underwear, but it paid the rent for a couple of weeks. Meeting Jacinta was another one of those magic moments in life where you know you have found someone special. She was sweet, naughty and she really made me laugh; still does.

I was starting to audition for a few acting jobs, but not having much luck. There were only so many free co-op plays at La Mama that I had left in me so I was starting to flirt with the idea of another career path. I had written a few plays at uni, so I considered going back and doing a year of Honours studies until I found my feet, but I decided to give acting and auditioning a full year of my attention, or maybe two, just to see if I could break into it. I had to fight feelings of frustration, which I know isn't unusual at the beginning of your career, but it did feel a bit like pushing shit uphill. I was pretty green as a performer, as most of my peers had been working in the industry since they were very young, so after a number of knockbacks I started to lose some confidence. I'd had rubbish thrown on me in the ocean in an ad to highlight the perils of littering, I'd taken a small role on *Australia's Most Wanted* and I was an extra on *Neighbours* for a day – but that was the extent of my CV. I wasn't sure what I could do to give myself a better chance at getting ahead.

I had given up the nightclub life and was folding cardigans for a living at Saba on Toorak Road, and making coffee in a cafe as a side hustle. At the same time, I was taking weekend drama classes and waiting by the phone after auditions for my agent to call, which she rarely did. A TV director, who was one of my coaches at drama class, took a shine to me and got me an audition for an episode of *Blue Heelers*. It was so exciting . . . until I received the call saying I didn't get the part. It was back in the days when your agent had to call to tell you that you didn't get a job and then was forced to awkwardly listen to your voice warble as you tried not to cry. *Nooooo, thhaaaaat's oooookkkkkkaaaaayyyy mmmaaaybbbeee neexxxtt tiiiiiimmme.*

Now they can just text or email and you can send a perky reply exclaiming how fine you are when you're actually holding back tears while opening the wine and chocolate. It's so much more humane for everyone involved.

During this time I met a guy called Kick Gurry in my drama class. We knew each other a tiny bit from around town; he seemed nice and we got along pretty well. I thought he was a good actor too and we did a couple of nice scenes together. We bonded when two people got up to do a scene and then just ended up dropping all of their lines making out on the floor in front of us for ten minutes. Were they method actors or just hot for each other? I guess we will never know, but it was awkward as hell. Meeting him didn't really feel like a big deal at the time, but it turned out it actually was.

◆

Amid the highs and lows of auditioning, my agent called one day to tell me I'd finally got my shot to audition for Jan Russ, a legend in the industry. I met Jan in 1997 when she was the casting director for *Neighbours*. She was known for discovering the likes of Kylie Minogue and Guy Pearce, among many others who went on to be big stars. Everyone knew who she was and most of us young actors in Melbourne wanted to get an audition with her. I was so nervous I worked on my scene all week – on the tram, in bed, I would even sneak into the backroom at work pretending to look for stock when really I was obsessively rehearsing.

When my audition day arrived I felt so nervous I wasn't sure if I was going to vomit or faint. I wasn't sure what kind of person would be waiting for me and to my surprise I was greeted by the friendliest, loveliest lady. She asked me about myself and I talked a million miles an hour (which I tend to do when I'm nervous), but I could tell that she warmed to me so I relaxed a little.

My audition wasn't very good, nerves got in the way – my voice was shaky and I could tell that I was a bit wooden. But I pushed through, because I read somewhere that actors shouldn't admit that they are nervous in auditions as it makes the person they are auditioning for question whether they could cope with the role. It was pretty obvious I couldn't cope with the role, though. I gave Jan a big grin at the end in the hope that my dazzling smile would distract her from my crappy performance, but her sweet look of encouragement betrayed her true thoughts. I was so used to performing in the theatre that I just wasn't camera-ready and I could tell that my lack of experience had let me down. I was surprised that I wasn't rushed out of the door and told never to return. But Jan stopped me to ask some questions then gave me advice about how to do better next time. 'I'll have you back,' she said, 'but go home and work on what I asked you to.' It was the first time that someone had shown blind faith in me, and after my years of flailing around in the wilderness working three jobs to make rent, I felt hope. I burnt every word Jan Russ said into my brain and I went home and worked and worked.

A few months later Jan had me back again and I felt like I did really well. She complimented me on my scene and told me she could see how hard I had been working. I really thought I had a shot. I didn't get that role, but my beautiful friend Diana Glenn did, so I couldn't be mad. Deep down I wasn't too disappointed because I felt confident she would invite me for another audition soon, which she did.

This time the role was more comedic, which suited me. I've always strived hard for naturalism in my performance and I had rehearsed every breath, every word to within an inch of its life so that I could go in and be truly messy and real. I like to run the lines incessantly so that when I approach the scene I can throw everything away and be free. I was still nervous, but being in a safe space allowed me to push through and perform a few of my tricks to the best of my ability. I think sometimes directors and auditioners can forget that to do our best work, actors need to be in a relaxed state so if they don't set up an environment where we feel supported it's hard to access our full potential.

The third time proved to be a charm! Jan Russ called me and said, 'We finally did it!' It was my very first proper paid acting role onscreen. No more folding cardigans and serving badly made cappuccinos.

It was heartwarming to have met such a champion of actors at the beginning of my career, when I was still a bit wonky on my feet. And I wasn't the only one who received this treatment, that's how Jan worked – she saw something in someone and then nurtured them until they were ready. That's a pretty amazing quality to have. There are a few 'Jans' out there in Australian casting and it makes the whole process so much more fulfilling, so much less traumatic. Because auditions can be brutal. Whenever I see Jan at an event she always proudly introduces me to people by saying, 'I gave Pia her first job!' It never ceases to be a thrill to be considered one of her many 'television children'.

◆

The role was fabulous and I'd grown up watching *Neighbours* so I was super excited to step on set and be a part of that beautiful piece of Australian history. I was lucky that Jacinta Stapleton was part of the cast, playing Amy – it was such a relief to know there would be a friendly face on set. Unfortunately she wasn't there on my first day of filming, so I was a lone soldier walking into battle.

I have a terrible sense of direction so TV studios have always been a terrifying place for me. They are huge rabbit warrens with endless hallways that all look exactly the same, and I have never been able to make sense of how to get to where I need to be without needing help. The initial challenge of that day was to actually find the green room, which was tucked away at the very back of the building. (I recently worked at the same studio and still got lost most days.) I took a breath and walked in fully prepared to be greeted by people I had only seen on screen, but not ready for how panicked it made me feel. In the moment before I walked into the green room, I wished with all my heart that I had chosen another career path, one in which I could seem cool, chill, at ease. *Just channel cool Pia, uber cool. Be calm, be calm, be* . . . 'OH HI!' I awkwardly blurted out over-enthusiastically to a lone actor sitting on a couch. He looked up at me and in my panic I rushed over to greet him a little too quickly and intensely, betraying all of my best laid plans. First days suck. Well, at least I wasn't wearing yellow banana shoes.

'I'm Pia!' I said and violently shoved my hand in the man's face, which he politely shook then introduced himself. While vigorously shaking his hand I bent down a little too far and at that exact moment, a tampon decided to fly out of my open bag and plop right into his lap. He stared at it lying motionless on his leg, then slowly pried his hand from my limp grip and picked up the small white object in his fingers.

'Would you like this back or was it a welcome gift?' he asked, which in hindsight is a very funny response, but I was too busy dying an internal death to notice.

'Oh, I'll take it back thanks,' I mumbled and then sat down, awkwardly smiling at him for the next twenty minutes until a makeup lady whisked him away to safety. He was lovely and would occasionally joke about what happened when we first met, but it definitely wasn't the start I had hoped for.

After he left I continued waiting on the couch. Two people came in and sat in front of me. They looked nice so, keen for my round two redemption story, I thought I'd stand up to greet them and went with the awkward, over-bubbly, 'Hi, I'm Pia!' again. I figured it might work better if I didn't throw a tampon at them. The young man smiled, but before he could speak the woman glared at me and said to him, 'My God, she's a bit cocky' and then laughed. She wrapped her arm around him and whispered something in his ear that I assumed was about me. I sat down and he went to talk, but she said, 'Don't speak to her.' I was so shocked that I went bright red in the face and was left to stare into my lap. This was before smartphones were able to divert us from mortifying humiliation so I just sat there with my shame until someone came and rescued me.

Luckily the rest of my time on the set of *Neighbours* turned out to be pretty great. I managed to get through my first scene without vomiting and although I was inexperienced, I could feel myself getting better and more confident every day. The worst thing about nerves is that sometimes they act as a brick wall between you and your ability; learning how to break down that wall can be hard. In the end it's really only time and experience that can do it. The directors were kind to me and my co-stars were lovely and really encouraging. The couch girl was only there for another month; though she managed to avoid speaking to me for the whole time. It was a bit peculiar, but I got over it.

The workdays on *Neighbours* were fast-paced and there wasn't much room for error, so when they said it was a good training ground for young actors, it's because it really was. Some of the older actors were especially supportive and encouraging (Tom Oliver was my favourite) and I got the sense that they appreciated the regular work even though it wasn't always completely stimulating. I learnt to keep my head down and work hard because at the end of the day the crew just want to get home in time for dinner.

It was strange ending up on a TV show that I watched as a kid. Walking around the sets and sitting in Lassiter's pub felt like I was living in some alternate universe and the sweet thrill of it was never lost on me. I had always dreamt of being in Hollywood musicals or working on Broadway, but *Neighbours* was actually a bucket list box ticked. I enjoyed every moment.

It was a great feeling not to be struggling for money. I appreciated being able to buy the nice bread from the deli and the fancy tampons (so I could throw them on people's laps in style). These were small things, but they meant a lot.

For that moment in time, my work life was great and things were feeling wonderful and light.

CHAPTER FOURTEEN

You're young if you're healthy,
and rich if you have no debts.
SICILIAN PROVERB

Strokes, aneurisms and heart attacks are the arseholes that like to turn up unannounced to throw people's lives into chaos. They are unfair and cruel and mostly come without warning. It starts as a normal day in which someone might get ready, have breakfast and go about their business unaware that this nasty visitor is about to arrive and change the world as you knew it. Some people are lost, some survive and some manage to overcome the challenges presented to them, perhaps coming to view them as a life-affirming experience. However, there is no denying that the shock is initially overwhelming and devastating and the aftermath is tough for everyone.

I was coming home from a long day at *Neighbours* when my phone rang from a private number. It was sometimes my agent so I picked it up excitedly in case Spielberg was calling. He wasn't. It was the hospital. Dad was in emergency after suffering a massive stroke. It sounded bad – his condition was critical, the serious voice on the phone told me – so I raced to emergency fearing the worst.

Everyone who has been through it knows that the drive to emergency is horrendous, but the stay in the waiting room is even worse. You sit there and analyse every look from the staff, every minute is excruciating, and life becomes clear, your needs become simple. It is incredibly scary, like horror movie scary, but you are inside the story, unable to escape.

I was the first one at the hospital, waiting for my sister, so I sat alone until someone came to speak to me. Dad had had two massive strokes, one after another, but somehow he had pulled through and survived.

If emergency departments are emotionally confronting places, ICU is worse. The days that roll into weeks, months and years become the new normal, but you know from the first time you walk in those doors that things will never be the same again. My father was in ICU for a few days and then transferred to a ward for over a month. During our time there I saw people die and heard their families' pain, but I also saw people get better and move on. Somehow time struggled on, and Dad slowly improved enough to be moved to rehab.

The stroke rehab ward was filled with people, young and old, who had all had their lives turned upside down by a singular event. There was a young guy in his twenties we got to know who'd had a stroke while playing cricket. He would never walk again, but his spirit was so strong and he was always chatting to everyone and cheering people up.

Another patient in rehab was a lovely lady who was so distressed most of the time and walked the halls all day and half of the night asking everyone, 'Have you seen my babies? Please, has anyone seen my babies?' She had no relief from her waking nightmare. Her babies were fine, they were adults who would come to visit her on weekends, but she didn't recognise them as her brain was stuck in a loop. She had been a successful businesswoman, but for some reason her body decided to force her to stop in the cruellest of ways and after a massive stroke, she was never the same. She would never find her babies and I could never forget her.

All of the religion and faith in God that I had been brought up with started to get muddled in my brain by witnessing these tragic stories. I was seeing the harsh reality that life was a cruel beast and that maybe the idea of God existed just so we didn't mentally and emotionally fall off a cliff. The more I let go of the idea of God, the more I started to drown in the horror of my own thoughts, because I was aware that no-one was protecting me. I was very much alone, in fact, we all were. It was a major existential crisis.

My dad was fifty at the time of his strokes, which is the age I am as I write these words. I always feared turning fifty because of this, but the truth is his life didn't end . . . it just changed. He became a person with a disability, but also a person who displayed an ability to overcome setbacks with a strong mental attitude. In stark contrast to how the experience affected my beliefs, he turned his second life into one that he embraced as a divine act of God's will.

Dad is in a wheelchair now and has one working arm. We sometimes joke about him starting a YouTube channel called 'Nonno Vinnie's One-Handed Tips for Singles' because he's always been very savvy about how to negotiate his disability. Taking lids off jars, peeling apples, putting on shoes. . . all of this became new again and so he had to problem-solve and work it out. Having a parent with a disability has taught me so much. I hadn't been aware before of the micro frustrations that happen every day when you are negotiating wheelchairs or an unsteady gait or other physical challenges in a world built solely for able-bodied humans. I can see now that we should be doing much better in society to be inclusive, but I was also proud of him for negotiating any roadblocks he faced.

◆

By this time, I was heading well into adulthood and beginning to worry a bit about my future. I was pretty sure I didn't have what it took to be a big Hollywood movie star, but I was still searching for something. I loved *Neighbours*, but I also wasn't sure if I wanted to stay there for the rest of my days. I didn't exactly know what my ultimate goal was; it felt just out of reach. I needed to learn to manage my expectations, but that's easier said than done.

CHAPTER FIFTEEN

If the devil pays you compliments, he wants your soul.

SICILIAN PROVERB

These days I tell my acting students to look in the mirror and determine what they most dislike about themselves, or the thing that they think is their biggest flaw, because that is the thing that is going to book them their first job and that is the thing that makes them special. The cruel twist about insecurity is that what we hate about ourselves is often what makes people fall in love with us. If only I had been able to tell my young self this. It would have saved me a lot of angst.

I sometimes felt a bit out of place in the acting world. I just wasn't prepared for the feelings of aesthetic inadequacy that I would have to battle in my career. I guess I was fairly happy, but like many actors the rejections and negative messages always rang louder in my head than the positives.

What I didn't know at the time was that there was a brilliant young woman called Melina Marchetta who had been writing a stunning piece of young adult fiction about a girl just like me, and because of her I was about to find my perfect fit. Melina is kind, clever, complicated and has a masterful understanding of character and story. She also grew up seeing herself in a similar way to how I did – just not quite fitting in.

After my nonna died and the Italian side of my family fell apart (Italians like to cut family off at the knees if they feel slighted), I was always looking to rediscover that world because I missed the richness of it. On the flip side, Melina's life was consumed by Italian culture, so her struggle was different from mine, but at the end of the day we shared that sense of not belonging. I channelled those feelings internally and questioned myself, whereas Melina transported those feelings into words and questioned the world around her.

Looking for Alibrandi was a story about an Italian–Australian girl searching for her identity. Even though it bizarrely wasn't snapped up by publishers immediately, she persisted and it was eventually released and became a massive hit. It has a notorious reputation for being the most stolen library book in the country and it touched the hearts of people all over the world.

It wasn't on my radar when it was first published, but if I had heard about it, I would have read it immediately. I was an obsessive devourer of novels, but I had never read a book in which I saw my own image and experience reflected back at me. *Looking for Alibrandi* was that book, but it passed me by. I guess when it ended up on the HSC curriculum it took on an even bigger life of its own, but I was about nineteen, out of school by then and focused on other things. When this brilliant novel ended up on my lap I was confused as to how it had escaped me.

Josie came into my life one sunny day as I was walking home to Elwood from St Kilda. I loved walking down buzzy Acland Street looking at all the cakes in the bakers' windows and browsing the bookstores. I remember being in a good mood as I walked past a cafe where my friend from my drama class, Kick Gurry, was sitting. He was furiously massacring a burger and looked slightly frazzled and unkempt. He lived nearby so it wasn't unusual to bump into him and have a chat. I stopped to say hi and he apologised sweetly for his manic state and subsequent burger abuse. He told me how he was auditioning for this movie about an Italian girl, which was stressing him out. He was the favourite for the role, but they couldn't find the lead actress and until they did they couldn't commit to him. He talked about how amazing the story was and I remember feeling a little jealous that he was going for movie roles, which seemed out of my league. I was lost in that thought when he said, 'Hey, she's Italian, you should go for it, you would be great!'

We had the same agent so I told him that if I was right for it, she probably would have sent me for an audition. I mentally let it go in that moment, wished Kick luck and said as chirpily as I could muster, 'I really hope you get it!'

I left Kick to finish off the burger and wandered back down the street toward home.

I walked in the door of my small second-floor flat with its parquetry floors and tiny balcony, and settled down in the sun with a book and a Nescafé Blend 43. I had a few weeks off *Neighbours* so I was enjoying the downtime with the security of knowing that I was back there in a few weeks. Almost as soon as I sat down, my phone rang. It was my agent.

'Look, there is a role that you might be right for, but you'll have to fly yourself to Sydney next week and put yourself up because they are worried you are too old.'

I wasn't really keen on blowing my money on a gamble, but she said it was a good project and might be worth it because they were getting desperate. They had been auditioning people all over Australia and couldn't find the lead so this was their last hurrah. She then told me it was for *Looking for Alibrandi*. I was immediately excited. I explained to her that I'd just seen Kick and I felt like maybe it was a sign. So I said I'd do it.

I borrowed Kick's copy of the book and swore to return it, which I never did. I went to bed early with the book that night, opened the pages and started to read . . .

'Panic was my first reaction to the multiple choice options that lay on my desk . . .' That is the moment my relationship with Josie began.

I remember feeling a weird sensation reading the book, like I had found my calling. I was trying to keep my emotions in perspective because auditioning is always a long shot and fraught with heartbreak, but I had a sense in my soul that it was meant to be. I was *meant* to play Josie. Old Catholic habits die hard so I started to pray to God to help me out. I was making deals all over the place. I didn't care what I had to do, I just needed to make it happen because I saw myself in Josie and I felt her in me; from the minute I picked up the book I felt like we were one.

I know I'm not the only one who felt this – so many girls connected with that incredible character. But as an actor, I had never had this feeling before – a sense of purpose and a laser-focused drive to make this character mine. I remember bingeing the book, not being able to move until I had read it all. When I'd finished I was filled with fear because it seemed like an impossible dream and I was already mourning the loss of the role. I knew I had to give it a shot, so I booked a ticket to Sydney.

◆

The auditions were held not far from the Harbour Bridge at Walsh Bay, in a huge warehouse space under the Sydney Theatre Company, which seemed impressive and highbrow, because it is. I walked in not sure what to expect and as I turned a corner, I was mortified to see hundreds of people waiting to go in. I realised then that I was in a cattle call audition, which is a horror I'd hoped I had left behind once my dancing days were over. My heart fell to the ground as it became apparent that I had wasted my time and my money.

I walked up to the check-in desk and a lovely lady said, 'Well, hello there, Pia, we've been expecting you.' I looked down as she grabbed a blurry picture of me dressed as a nun (another sign) that had been taken at a casting for a car ad months before. 'I'm glad you made it,' she said as she stuck a number on my chest. I mentally held onto her friendly greeting as a trinket to help me find the courage to get through the day. It was hard when there were hordes of girls who looked just like me. I usually felt like I stood out a little at auditions, but here I felt invisible among a sea of Italian-looking girls, all dying to be Josie.

All the Josies were herded into a large room like cattle about to be slaughtered, and I guess we kind of were, because that's how auditions like this work. They are horrible and weird, but understandably necessary. Basically, a group of people perform a task and then afterwards you wait for someone to call your number. If your number is called you get to go to the next round and if it isn't, you are going home to cry. If you have ever watched the movie *A Chorus Line* or any other show that pits a group of artists against each other, you get the vibe. I found out that they were not only looking for Josie, but also an actor for the role of Sera, Josie's best friend and flirting with a few possible Carly Bishops, even though Leeanna Walsman had apparently already been cast.

As I walked into that room I saw three women sitting at a table. Director, producer, writer. I caught the eyes of one woman and tried to melt her heart with a dazzling smile; she stared right through me. Afterwards I found out that this was Melina and she had been instructed not to smile at any of the actors. She later told me that she found that really hard to do, but I didn't know that at this stage, so I just decided that she must have hated me on sight.

The first task was a movement piece, where we had to walk into the middle of the room one by one and pretend we had entered a sacred space. I was hoping to use some of my dance prowess to impress them, but my moment in the sun only lasted for five seconds so I really wasn't sure how I was going to stand out. When that exercise was over we all had to sit down and after much discussion between the three women the numbers were read out. When I heard mine I was overjoyed, but I looked around at the huge group of Josies who were left and I knew I still had a massive job ahead of me.

The day was long and my memory of it is a blur because it was so intense. There was lots of standing around waiting and then having to turn on a performance or a mood to show you had what it took. After hours of torturous competition and nervous tension, the last two numbers were read out. Mine was one of those numbers. There we were, two of us: a curly-, brown-haired girl and me.

I was trying to be pleasant to my rival, but I was internally comparing myself to her and plotting ways to make myself the victor in this race. Josie felt so close, but I knew I still had a huge mountain to climb. Then the friendly lady from the beginning of the day handed us both a script and told me I would be reading for the part of Josie and the curly-, brown-haired girl she would be reading for the part of Sera. Everything went quiet. I could hear the pounding of blood pumping in my ears and I had an overwhelming desire to run. The three stoic women behind the desk took down their barriers and introduced themselves. They were kind and chatty and very nurturing. The director, Kate Woods, introduced herself then handed me a script that I was going to have to cold read in front of everyone. This was not one of my strengths. I tried to look calm, took a breath and read the lines. Then the girl going for Sera did hers. We were both clearly nervous, but neither of us totally sucked, which was a bonus.

I had a thick set of bangs and they asked me to pull my fringe back so they could see my face, then took a few polaroids of me. I hoped I didn't look like an egghead.

It wasn't over yet. I was asked to sit down alone in a big room with the three women and they asked me questions about myself and ballet and my family. They wanted to get an idea of who I was. I tried to answer them without looking like a deer in headlights. The truth was, I was still trying to work it out myself and rediscover who I was, so I wasn't sure I could give them what they wanted.

Though they were encouraging, I could tell they were unsure about the person who lay underneath the exterior I was presenting and whether I had the depth to be the person they needed me to be to bring Josie to life. I can sense sometimes when people meet me that there is a frustration that they can't get more, or they sense a facade. I think I'm just emotionally reserved around new people, and I use humour and try to be disarming to deflect scrutiny in those situations.

I sat on that small chair in the middle of this huge room for what seemed like an eternity and then finally the director handed me a photocopied excerpt from the novel and said they'd like me to improv it. I relaxed a little as improv had always been a love and strength of mine. I hoped that I would nail it even though I had an overwhelming feeling that they were going to break my heart. I looked at the page – it was the moment that Josie talked to Jacob about how angry she was about John's death. I could tell they wanted to see if I could transcend what was on the page and find the core truth of the character, rather than just see 'acting'. All I could think was, 'Oh shit, this is going to be hard.'

I looked down at the page with a lump in my throat, trying to remember my yoga breathing and not hyperventilate. It was such a beautifully written scene, I felt if I just looked inward I might have a fighting chance.

The lines read: 'You know something, Jacob, I'd hate to be as smart as John. I mean he was really, really smart and to be that smart means you know all the answers, and when you know all the answers there's no room for dreaming.' The words were so powerful to me. Suddenly, I thought maybe I didn't need to be great to get this part, maybe I just needed to let go and be Josie.

As I sat in my chair waiting for my next instruction, they told me they had someone to read with me. The door opened and Kick strolled in. He was looking scruffy in a good way, wearing a faded singlet and some ripped Diesel jeans. He looked cute, slightly hungover, his hair was a mess and, well, he was basically Jacob. In that moment he was also my saviour.

Kick has an excitable swagger and a way about him that is endearing and disarming; it's basically hard to be stressed around him. His energy is light, but he has a depth, so working with him has always been effortless and fun.

Kick smiled and sat down next to me. They instructed us to read the scene from the book and then improv a conversation about John's death. Kate said, 'When a friend dies you can feel angry and let down so talk about that to each other, but as Josie and Jacob.' We looked at each other and began reading the scene. Then we broke away from the script and I looked in his eyes and thought about all of the hurt and pain that comes with losing a friend. I thought of Marcus and his car accident and how mad I was at him and the world and at myself for being such an arsehole before he died, and I turned him into John Barton in my brain and I let go.

I don't know what I said, I don't know what Kick said, but we were Jacob and Josie in that moment, and it was sad and painful and real. At the end of it he put his arms around me and said, 'It's okay, it's okay.' I sobbed and sobbed in his arms until Kate said, 'Cut.' She walked over to me, hugged and kissed me, and with tears in her eyes said, 'I've found you, I've found you.'

CHAPTER SIXTEEN

I'm beginning to realise that things don't turn out
the way you want them to. And sometimes when
they don't, they can turn out a little better.

JOSIE ALIBRANDI

There is a joke among actors that the best part of getting
a job is hearing the good news and the worst part is when
you realise you actually have to do the work. I don't ever
mind the work, but the waiting kills me. After the exhilaration of the audition process, then receiving some texts
telling me that I was Josie, I had to wait almost six months
to receive official confirmation that I definitely had the role
and to learn the start date for filming. Kick was in the
same predicament. During those months I checked my
phone ten times a day. I kept expecting the worst. Maybe
the production team lost funding? Maybe we were recast?
Maybe they changed their mind about me? I didn't know,

Kick didn't know and our agent didn't know, so we just waited and waited.

It seemed *Looking for Alibrandi* had turned into *Waiting for Anthony* because Anthony LaPaglia was the reason we were in limbo. He was so busy that his availability couldn't be confirmed and until it was, the production was stalled. Kate, the director, said they couldn't make the movie without him, and they were right.

So we waited and waited, and then the calls came. I was officially offered the role of Josie, Kick was offered the role of Jacob, and Dan Spielman was offered the role of John. I think we were all relieved rather than elated because the wait had been torture. Anthony still wasn't available for a few more months so the producers decided to put us into a sort of acting bootcamp. We did workshops and studied with amazing coaches like Lindy Davies and Nico Lathouris, who is one of the most interesting and energised dramaturgs that I have ever worked with. I loved working with Nico, he never let me off the hook and for someone like me, who can feel compelled to hide in high-intensity situations, he was the perfect teacher.

I headed to Sydney for the bootcamp with so much excitement in my heart, but it was tempered by an inner fear that they would change their minds and fire me. Someone once told me they can't fire you after two weeks of filming anything, so I have never relaxed until that two weeks is up. Never. I recently heard about someone getting fired from a TV job three weeks after filming began, so that theory is clearly wrong. I guess I'll never learn to breathe easy. Regardless of my inner turmoil, I was completely enjoying the energy of embarking on something huge and meaningful.

Because I was hired as a Sydney-based actor, my accommodation costs weren't covered by the production – I had to find my own board. In a stroke of luck, Nicole was living in Sydney at the time so I stayed with her, which was comforting. It was nice to spend time with my sister and have a home to come back to at the end of each day.

I spent a lot of time at the director Kate Wood's house, bonding, watching movies and talking about Josie. Kate loves actors – I could tell she was going to hold my hand through the whole thing. She promised me that together we wouldn't leave a fake moment on screen, that everything we did would be real and truthful. She became my friend, mother, mentor, annoying older sister all wrapped up in one, and it still remains the most special working relationship I have ever had.

We all spent time at the home of Melina Marchetta's grandmother, eating Italian food and hanging out with her family. I loved being welcomed by this Italian tribe, where the table settings were festive, the food was mouth-watering and little familiar quirks like crocheted doilies and pictures of the Virgin Mary decorated the room, just like at Nonna's. It was that Italian family vibe I had so missed and almost forgotten about; now here I was making a film about identity, and rediscovering who I was in the process.

To be welcomed into a new Italian family after somewhat losing mine and then showered with so much love was an amazing feeling. It rekindled my connections to my Italian heritage, which I had set aside after Nonna's death and so I started to love that part of myself again. It was wonderfully cathartic because I had all but left that world behind me to avoid the sadness I felt when I thought about it. When I started to understand my grief, the healing began. I knew I was going to be changed forever after this film, I just wasn't sure how yet.

◆

Everyone involved in making this movie knew we were making something special, so we left our old lives at the door and created a new one for this short, magical period of time. We were in it for the love, definitely not the money – most of us didn't walk away with much income from this work – but we knew it was about more than that. We created a new family, and when Greta Scacchi and Anthony LaPaglia eventually joined us, we were complete. It seemed like an eternity to get there but once everyone had arrived, it felt so right.

Leeanna Walsman was cast as Carly, Josie's nemesis, and we became fast friends. I didn't really know anyone in Sydney and so it was nice to make a good friend so quickly and easily. We hung out a lot outside of filming and we eventually became flatmates so it was a lucky break having my good friend play my nemesis. The only hiccup in the casting was that when we got to Sydney, Dan was deeply immersed in a play he was performing in and then he was gone. After months of him being John Barton in my head and heart, he had suddenly disappeared. When we found out he'd left the production, Kick and I were devastated. Dan was unique and perfect for the role of John, with his deep soulful energy and intellectual demeanour and he seemed irreplaceable. It was poignant that fictional John broke fictional Josie's heart by leaving her, and Dan leaving broke mine, so I packed it away to use later.

Auditions for a new John were held, and it was was hard for me to mentally embrace someone else so quickly, but at the end of the day, Matt Newton won the role. His was a completely different take on the character, one that was filled with a lightness and confidence that worked. This was only a week before shooting began so it was a lot to digest, but when he joined the cast it felt complete again and we started to have fun.

One of the great things about the job was working with Anthony and Greta, who played my parents. Greta has a way about her that makes you instantly relaxed and calm, she is a true earth mother, so creating a loving mother–daughter relationship with her was more than easy. Her slow, graceful pace always made me feel centred and warm, so she naturally brought out the best in me when I was acting opposite her. Greta just gets how to connect with people, so all of our onscreen moments felt genuine.

And then there was Dad. Anthony is one of those people who likes to take young actors under his wing and pass on his wisdom to help them along their path. He did that for me. He is an all-in passionate actor and he was more than generous in his mentorship – constantly giving me tips and teaching me things to ensure that we did the best work that we possibly could. Basically he was a dream to work with. Kate seemed to think I had a crush on him, because in scenes she kept laughing and yelling out, 'Don't forget, he is your father!' The truth was, I was just felt very buoyant when I was in his presence, because I knew he was making me a better actor and I was so grateful for his generosity. He is handsome, though.

◆

Kate was really the matriarch of the whole project, she held it together, and we all knew we were in good hands. It was all humming along nicely; we were consumed by the work and weren't thinking about anything outside of it.

We had become the characters, and an instant family, and we were obsessive and passionate about creating a great piece of work. Because Kick and I weren't from Sydney and we had missed the hype of the book, we didn't actually realise what a massive deal this movie was. As we were shooting, we slowly started to understand that it was a book people were completely obsessed with – it felt thrilling and a bit intimidating to be bringing that story alive. But it wasn't until we filmed the 'Have a Say Day' scene at the Opera House that we realised our lives were about to change. 'Have a Say Day' is a huge moment in the narrative where Josie and Jacob meet during a youth public speaking event. For fans of *Looking for Alibrandi*, it was a hugely exciting thing to be a part of. There were so many extras there on the day, as well as a crowd of hundreds, and when we came on set, people lost their minds, screaming, 'OMG, it's Jacob and Josie.' The crowd was shouting out our character names and a girl cried when she met me. I remember Kick saying to me, 'I think this is going to be bigger than we thought.' He was right. It was a brief insight into what was to come for us.

I know this all sounds like a lovefest, and I guess it kind of was. At the end of the day, Melina and Kate set the tone for everything that happened on set, and I have to say it was a blessing and a curse to have such an incredibly positive and artistically satisfying experience in my first big job. Every moment was precious. I became so immersed in Josie's world and in Melina's story that I truly felt like I was Josie; she had changed my DNA. We were one and the same. When it ended it was bittersweet because I simultaneously lost a part of myself, but I had also gained something momentous.

The work days were long and I didn't have a scene off, so I was constantly exhausted, but buoyed by the excitement. I couldn't believe how lucky I was. I fluctuated between feeling like I didn't deserve it and knowing that I was born to be Josie. I was so deep in it, we all were. If Kate talked about John's death I would burst into tears, because even though I knew it wasn't real, my emotions were. That is the beauty of Melina's writing – the characters might be fictional, but they are alive in our hearts. I tried to take in every moment, every trip over the Harbour Bridge, every time someone said, 'Cut', every conversation, every take. I wanted to bottle it up and live within those moments forever because I was so overcome with the experience. I never wanted it to end. I never wanted to say goodbye to Josie, and in a weird way I never had to because, I suspect, for the rest of my days, people will see her when they look at me.

But filming had to end. I didn't want to go to the wrap party because I was feeling empty and overwhelmed and sad, but Kate reminded me that I had a responsibility to be gracious. She was absolutely right. It was a magic time of learning and getting to know some terrific people, and though it was coming to a close, saying goodbye to it all was a part of honouring what we had shared.

I was going to end this chapter there, but I have a very firm request from Kick that I mention in this book the fact we made out at the aforementioned party, and to let you know that he was a great kisser. There you go, Kick; a perfectly sweet way to end a chapter about a perfect time in our lives. Life imitating art . . . for a minute, anyway.

CHAPTER SEVENTEEN

Open my heart and you will see,
graved inside of it, Italy.

ROBERT BROWNING

I first went to Italy when I was five years old, and I still remember it clearly, because even at that young age I knew it was magical. We had taken Nonna back to the Aeolian Islands to see family and we were constantly surrounded by great food and happy people. It felt like a second home to me. I couldn't understand what anyone was saying, but it didn't matter because I could feel the love. It was alarmingly bright and steaming hot, but we were surrounded by the blue Tyrrhenian Sea that would generate a soft breeze to cool our skin. It was a place frozen in time with old-world interiors that were simple and inviting with basic amenities, like a hole in the ground for a toilet. I'm pretty sure there wasn't a television, but if there was I don't remember it. Most evenings a man would wander the streets ringing a bell and people would come out to buy a few slices of fresh swordfish that he would cut off on the spot for our dinner. I found it so thrilling when he would walk up our street because it was like an ice-cream truck but with fish. I love fish. Nonna and her sister would come inside and make some pesce fritto with some fresh vegetables from the garden and we would feast on all of the colourful delights. There was always fresh bread to soak up the juices of your meal (dipping bread in sauce is still one of my favourite things) and lots of fruit from the garden to eat. Even then, in my tiny kid brain, I felt like I was living in a movie.

I love the simplicity of a traditional Italian backyard that is all about practicality rather than aesthetics. The Italian garden ethos is if you can't grow fruit on it then you concrete over it. I grew up around gardens with lots of concrete, fruit trees and tomato plants and it always makes me happy to see that combination. Put a Hills hoist in the middle of the garden for good measure and I am actually in Australian–Italian heaven. Okay, so there were no Hills hoists in Italy, but there was definitely lots of fruit and concrete.

I passed the time in Lipari by playing with my cousin. He spoke no English and I spoke no Italian, but we made it work. We created our own cute language and would babble on to each other for hours and hours as we played on the street and got into mischief. Everyone thought we were so sweet together, and some of the aunts started plotting our wedding. 'Oh, these two are going to get married,' they would say. I held onto the idea for years, thinking I might go back to the islands to marry my cousin. It's a small island with slim pickings, so it wasn't an outrageous thought to marry your cousin, but I eventually worked out that it probably shouldn't be my destiny. I stand by the fact that he was adorable, though.

I remember Nonna being so happy and animated while we were in Italy, and I clung onto her constantly during that trip because the essence of her was everywhere and the joy that surrounded us was intoxicating. I never wanted to leave the islands, I was so happy there, barefoot in the sun surrounded by the busy family energy. My whole life, all I ever wanted was to go back there and feel that connection to the sand and volcanoes. I have always been drawn to the sun and the sea, and I think there is something about that time and those people that I needed to revisit to accept who I am, to understand something that is so potent in my blood, but also remains a mystery.

◆

I had always wanted to go back to Italy and the most beautiful and unexpected surprise about *Looking for Alibrandi* was that we were invited to go to Taormina in Sicily for a film festival. The organisers of the Taormina

Film Festival were flying Kate, Melina and me over from Australia, all-expenses paid, and putting us up in a beautiful hotel. We were meeting Greta and her family there so we were going to have a mini reunion in paradise. I literally could not believe my luck, it was so unbelievably exciting. We flew business class, which I had never done before, so I was totally overstimulated by the free food, movies and champagne. (Being overexcited by free food is a common theme for me.)

It was the most amazing moment when I stepped off the plane at Rome airport. I looked around at all of the people and I saw myself; young women who looked like me were literally everywhere in the airport crowd. I hadn't expected to be so emotional. That overwhelming sense of belonging is how most people must feel when they return to a country where their heritage reflects their physicality. I've always joked that I don't want to take my husband to Italy because he will realise how unremarkable I am, though.

The very first thing I did when my feet hit the ground was order an espresso from the airport cafe. I just stood there alone, staring at everyone, trying not to cry with happiness. I was a tiny bit hungover from the free business class champagne, so that probably added to my delicate emotional state, but it was still a great experience.

Kate, Melina and I then continued on to Taormina, which meant taking another flight to Catania. I'm not a great flyer at the best of times, but I found it more than a little scary when everyone started praying as we were landing. I had a mild panic then joined in. I later discovered that it's an Italian tradition to pray on flights, so I'm glad I didn't start screaming and try to jump out the window, which was my overwhelming instinct at the time.

Catania airport wasn't easy to navigate, but eventually we found our way to Taormina, which was one of the most beautiful places I had ever visited. To top it all off, the whole town was abuzz and filled with activity as the film festival guests had taken over. Our social calendar was immediately full, with dinners and parties, but we also had plenty of time to wander the streets to take in the picturesque town and meet the lovely locals. There was a cute little fruit shop near my hotel that a sweet nonna ran, and she would sit outside on a milk crate, chatting to everyone. I would wander there most days to talk to her in my terrible attempt at Italian, which she seemed to find amusing. She was so friendly and oddly reminded me of home. I would buy pistachio nuts and peaches from her that I would happily snack on throughout the day until it was time to go to the dinners and parties that went well into the early morning.

This trip was my first, and definitely most exotic, experience of being chaperoned by a film festival and I loved being treated to expensive dinners and exclusive black tie parties – I'm glad I lapped up every minute. I guess some actors do this stuff all the time, but I never really felt like it was my destiny, so I knew I should take in every moment. I managed to get into a mild amount of mischief with some English girls I met and spent a very late night in a local bar where men bought us wine and hit on us in a fairly innocent kind of way. I skipped home after midnight where one of the festival workers saw me walking down a deserted street, picked me up in her car and berated me in Italian for walking alone. She was probably right, but it seemed like a harmless little town and I hadn't realised it was not seen as appropriate for a young woman in southern Italy to engage in late-night solo walks after a couple of vinos. Anyway, I nodded and apologised in bad Italian and she dropped me off at my hotel, where I went back to my room and binged on pistachios and watched dubbed Italian movies until I fell asleep. How fun.

◆

Greta Scacchi met us at the festival and as always she was such fun to be around. We would sit together in her room sipping champagne or drinking espresso as she entertained me with colourful stories about Hollywood, most of which were cautionary tales wrapped up in hilariously comedic anecdotes. Greta is an incredibly funny and witty human and she is also a great supporter of women. I hung out with her children, who I fell instantly in love with, and

I felt part of her family for a short while. Just like on the film set, I noticed the world seemed to slow down when Greta was around. People in Italy stared adoringly at her or opened restaurants that were closed to make us feasts, letting us luxuriate for as long as we wanted. Her beauty captivated everyone, but it was her presence that was really intoxicating; people gravitate toward her. I loved watching this Italian movie star stroll the streets of Italy oblivious to the effect she had on the world. Greta was so kind when we were at parties and she graciously introduced me to Italian filmmakers like Michelangelo Antonioni and Hollywood types who I would never have dreamt of meeting. Just as our trip was ending, Greta had organised for us to all go to another film festival in Rome – I was excited to extend my trip because I wasn't ready for it to be over.

Thanks to Greta, we were able to enjoy a blissful summer in Rome. I got to see the sights, and eat different pistachio-flavoured treats and creamy gelato (vanilla with chunks of fresh cherries was my favourite). The weather was so hot so I loved to cool down with copious amounts of cafe granita that gave me caffeine-induced heart palpitations. I ate delicious pasta for every meal and more than my weight in cannoli. I adored Rome and all of the religious history to be found. Its impressive statues and grand, violent art made me feel small among its majesty. It reminded me of being at my aunts' houses, surrounded by religious paintings while they performed mini exorcisms on me and my sister. Ahhh, the memories.

I managed to get kicked out of the Sistine Chapel for wearing a singlet, which made me wonder if the aunts were right all along? Maybe I actually was cursed and unworthy of entering such a holy space. Despite the spiritual freakout that it gave me, the visit wasn't a total loss because I got a refund on my ticket by arguing that they should have some 'no shoulders allowed' signs at the entrance. I don't want to start a beef with the Sistine Chapel and end up going to hell, but we manage the no thongs signs at local RSLs in Australia – it's just a suggestion. (This was a long time ago so maybe things have changed? Someone check for me and report back please.) Anyway, I went out and bought a novelty Vatican t-shirt that covered my shoulders, then went back for round two so I could see the chapel in peace, without guards threatening to arrest me.

Afterwards, I went to St Peter's Basilica and popped into confession to beg for forgiveness, as my singlet drama was annoyingly weighing on my mind. The priest told me I was lucky to have found God today and asked if I had any other sins to confess. 'Hmmm, let's say everything, but not murder,' I replied. He gave me a penance of five Hail Marys and then told me my soul would be clean. Wow, that was easy; I like being Catholic. Note to self: must go to confession once a year.

I found Rome to be one of those travel experiences that I had always wished for. Lots of food, fun, a smattering of religious history and the faintest essence of coming home. Hanging out with Greta, Kate and Melina was the icing on the cake; it felt like a family holiday and a fitting end to the long and wonderful journey we had all been on together.

◆

I had managed to make some new friends on my trip, which added to the joy of the whole experience. When I was in Taormina, I met a lovely guy called Z who had seen *Looking for Alibrandi* and loved it, so we swapped details. He told me he worked in films and he wanted to catch up while I was in Rome, show me around, introduce me to some film people and take me to his favourite restaurants. Sign me right up. When you are doing the festival circuit it's not unusual to be hosted by people from film companies at dinners, drinks or events, and you can bond quickly, because you are all connected by a passion for film and the thrill of being a part of the industry you love. I was eager to hang out.

On the first night Z and I went out, he popped me on the back of a Vespa, which made me feel like I was Audrey Hepburn in *Roman Holiday*. I'm not overly romantic; in fact, I really, really hate romantic comedies, or romance in general, but something about an Italian man driving me around Rome on his Vespa touched a dormant whimsical part of my heart. He took me out for beautiful dinners and we hung out with his friends, and a couple of gorgeous female Italian models who were very sweet and tried to teach me the language over pasta and wine. He knew lots of people and one night we met up with Harvey Weinstein, who was also in Italy for the festivals. This was exciting for me because my love for *The Talented Mr Ripley* runs deep. Harvey seemed very friendly. He was quite sexually rambunctious in his conversation topics, but I was more bemused than concerned by it, because he was just very jovial and friendly.

'Go home and have sex with Z, he loves you!' he exclaimed one night. 'He wants to marry you and move you to Rome, you have to go and sleep with him tonight! You Australian girls are wild in bed, it's all whips and chains. Go have fun.' I told him whips and chains were not my thing, and it did start to get a bit uncomfortable at that point, but he seemed harmless. Plus, he didn't drink – I was used to drunk and sleazy bosses from working in pubs and nightclubs, so I wasn't so uneasy.

Z did seem to like me and we'd shared a few moments back at his flat, but he just wasn't quite my type even though he had a certain charm. In the end, I decided I didn't want to sleep with him . . . so I didn't. He was nice about it and let it go.

Greta wasn't a fan of my trips out with Z. She told me a few cautionary stories about Hollywood, but this was a friend of the head of a massive film company and Z was really nice, so I assumed she was being overprotective. One night when I was making my way out to dinner with him, Greta demanded to see his business card. Waving it in my face, she told me not to trust these men and that she wanted me to have dinner with her and the kids instead. I was touched by how sweet she was to worry about me, but I was having fun and Z didn't give me bad vibes, so off I went. Greta didn't seem convinced, but I was confident I was nailing this 'when in Rome' life.

Eventually, Z started to get the hint that he had been put in the 'friend zone' and although I still saw him socially, his interest waned. I was conscious of remaining friendly and charming around him and Harvey, though, because that's how actors often are to people in power, it's how we hustle for jobs. Auditions, dinner meetings, film festival parties are all set up to give actors the opportunity to dazzle strangers into giving us work, so in those situations I would put my sparkliest persona on to try to tap-dance my way to victory.

Just before I was due to leave for London, Z said it could be fun for me to fly there on a private jet with Harvey. I had never been on a private jet before and I was pretty sure I'd seen a picture in a magazine of Penelope Cruz on this exact jet, but a few things made me hesitate. My dislike of small planes, for one, but also the worry that it could all fall over at the last minute, leaving me stranded. I was already booked on a nice, safe British Airways flight to London. My hesitation became even more pronounced when my hotel room phone began ringing incessantly – Harvey and Z were calling me non-stop, trying to convince me to go. Then Z let slip that Harvey and I were going to be alone on the plane, which just seemed stressful. Was that going to be like a three-hour audition? Geez, I didn't know if I had the stamina to be charming for three hours. I figured that must be a pretty standard event in their world and, even though I was worried about keeping up a decent conversation for that long, I thought I shouldn't be rude. I decided I'd let Greta know I was changing my travel plans.

I skipped down to Greta's room, excited for us to spend our last day in Rome together. But when I told her I might fly to London with Harvey Weinstein on his private jet, she wasn't having any of it. She flew into a panic, and told me that I shouldn't do it. I told her it was arranged and that a car was coming for me that evening. Greta demanded that I cancel.

'Something bad will happen to you on that plane,' she warned me. She walked with me back to my room, where my phone was still ringing, and she took it off the hook, watched me finish packing and got the film festival to book me a car so I could make my original flight. She actually advised me to catch a train, because she said the drivers were terrifying in Italy, but I was tired and kind of annoyed about her disconnecting my phone, so I insisted I would take the car. She was right again. The driver ended up taking me to the back of Rome airport and asking me in Italian to give him a blow job, which took a bit of back and forth between us until I understood what he wanted. Though the abandoned field where he stopped the car while sporting a huge grin on his face was kind of a giveaway. Then he unbuttoned his pants and I definitely understood what he wanted. He ended up being very apologetic and blamed the language barrier – he thought I had offered him one. The Italian word for blow job is *pompino* and on reflection, he did seem overly excited when I mentioned I had been to Pompeii. It could have been that? Perhaps I was being too forgiving. Anyway, when I emphatically denied this, he sheepishly drove me to departures.

I finally made it safely to Heathrow on a big, safe commercial jet. I felt a bit guilty that I had been rude to Harvey Weinstein, but I reassured myself that he seemed to really like my work and we had a decent rapport, so I was sure I'd get the opportunity to audition for one of his films soon. As it turns out, I never did, but I'm fine with it because nothing terrible happened to me either. Sure, maybe nothing bad would have happened to me on that plane alone with him, but after so many brave women spoke up about him over the years, I'm grateful I never got to find out.

My encounter always seemed fairly tame in my head, although after the stories surrounding Harvey Weinstein started to come out, my time with Harvey seemed a little heavier. Then one day I was lying in bed when my husband walked in with an article on his phone. He said, 'Look at this.'

I saw the headline and my heart dropped a little. I read the article and it dropped further. It detailed how Z allegedly hunted for young actresses at Italian film festivals to deliver to Harvey Weinstein as playthings. There were actresses with stories similar to mine: the wining and dining, the incessant phone calls, private jet rides . . . all of it. The difference for me was that I had someone looking out for me, so I had escaped unscathed. There was another article that was even more disturbing. I realised that I was almost delivered like a meal on a platter and served on a private jet to Harvey Weinstein.

I know that people like to judge young women who get themselves into compromising positions because 'they should have known better', but the truth is no, we shouldn't. We shouldn't need to be suspicious and on guard when we are young, vulnerable and ambitious. Every meeting is thrilling, every encounter with people who make brilliant films is a highlight because when you passionately love movies, you want to be surrounded by people who feel the same. Even though I knew I was no Gwyneth Paltrow, I would constantly wonder what it would be like to have a small part in a Miramax film. It didn't seem unrealistic during that stint in Rome that film executives would be talking to me about future work, because I was at the beginning of a promising career and I was filled with hope. But I was duped. Harvey Weinstein wasn't a fan of my work, I was just a disposable young woman who was easy prey.

When you are an actress, you are surrounded by people who have power over your career. Some of those people are wonderful and some are not. I was lucky not to learn that lesson the hard way back then. For years, I recalled what I thought was an innocent holiday adventure with a nice guy who drove me around on the back of a Vespa when the reality was something far more sinister.

I'm sorry for all the women who suffered at Weinstein's hands or went through terrible things at the hands of other men who haven't faced their reckoning yet. To all those women I say, you deserve better and our daughters deserve better. I'm sorry for everyone who didn't have a Greta and I hope to always be a Greta to other young women until I no longer need to be.

Greta Scacchi is the hero of this story and forever a hero of mine.

PART THREE

PART THREE

CHAPTER EIGHTEEN

Wisdom is the daughter of experience.

DANTE ALIGHIERI

I was on a high after Italy. It was a bonus that I didn't know what I'd narrowly avoided, so my exuberance and enthusiasm were undimmed. I decided I would try LA out after London. Not because I had much desire to work there – as I've said, I already had the feeling Hollywood wasn't going to be for me – but because my agents were keen for me to give it a shot. This was before smartphones and virtual auditions, so I decided I would go so that I could say I tried. Mostly I just wanted to visit Disneyland, shop at Urban Outfitters and try an In-N-Out burger, which all turned out to be excellent choices. I also shopped some great vintage clothes with friends, but ended up eating my burgers alone, because carbs were apparently out of fashion.

I did have some memorable film-world experiences while I was there, though. I was lucky enough to have a meeting with Oscar-winning director Anthony Minghella in a vibey hotel cafe. He was kind and respectful and talented. I don't think he was seriously considering me for the film we were meeting about, but he generously feigned interest in my life, asking me questions about myself and listening intently. He gave me some insights into how he made films. We had a few laughs and it was such a positive experience that I walked away feeling inspired. I didn't get the role, but I didn't really care and just felt lucky to have met him. Particularly since he died tragically young, aged fifty-four. What a loss.

Amazingly, I also scored an audition with Wes Craven, and even though I was extremely nervous because I'm a massive fan, he laughed at my jokes and was so encouraging that I managed to pull off a pretty good audition. Halfway through, though, my earring got caught in my lacy top and I had to yell out for help. He leapt out of his chair like a superhero to save me from this hilariously humiliating event. It took two whole minutes to unravel that earring. He chatted and laughed the whole way through it, which turned my embarrassment into an anecdote I've dined out on at parties ever since. I didn't get the role, but I didn't really care and just felt lucky to have met him.

Then I met Steven Bochco, the creator of *Hill Street Blues*, *Doogie Howser M.D.*, *L.A. Law* and *NYPD Blue* among other major TV series, in an audition. He was surprisingly low-key and incredibly interesting. I walked away from that audition feeling good about myself, and later received a few callbacks and came close to booking the job. I didn't get the role but I didn't really care and just felt lucky to have met him.

I found it was easier not to care about booking jobs in these instances because meeting wonderfully creative people who were so warm and generous was such a thrill for me, a young actress in a world that seemed full of possibilities.

Not surprisingly, though, not every LA audition was all wine and roses. I don't want to be rude, but in my opinion there are some real twits running that town. I went to one audition where I opened my mouth and said the first sentence of a scene only to have the man auditioning me put his hand in my face and yell, 'You aren't funny!' I thought, *I am fucking funny, thanks buddy,* but I didn't say it. I just smiled and thanked him for the time as his assistant ushered me out of the room. Surprise, surprise – I didn't get the role.

I went for another role in a vampire film and the man auditioning me berated me for not being sexy. He kept making large circular motions around his chest area and saying, 'You need to find your womanly sexiness, you need to be sexier.' By that point, I was kind of jack of LA, and I sarcastically asked him what I should do to enable him to find me sexy. 'Are you telling me I need bigger tits?' I asked with a smile on my face and daggers in my eyes.

'That's your choice,' he replied smugly but I could tell he was saying yes. *Okay, thanks dude.* As I left I told him I'd look into it. I didn't.

Later that same week I went for a role in a teen film and as I was heading through the waiting area to go to my audition an older, very famous movie star strolled past me with his entourage. He stopped me, gently held my arm and said, 'You are so fucking hot.' I went red and awkwardly smiled as his gang of assistants giggled encouragingly. As I walked away, he said loudly, 'Oh my God, you have a great arse too.' I entered that audition feeling a bit disconcerted, but not overly alarmed because apparently my arse was great – and a compliment is a compliment.

I stood at the front of the room ready to give a great read. The room was intimidating because it was huge and empty, and I was standing alone at one end while a surly looking lady stood at the other with an uninterested look on her face. But I had worked really hard on the screen-test and I felt pretty confident I could deliver. I gave myself an internal pep talk, *You are going to nail this, P!* I smiled and took a deep breath.

'What role are you reading for?' the surly woman said in a thick New York accent. I told her the name of the role and she said, 'WHAT?' So I repeated myself. She looked at me mortified and said, 'But that's the role of the hot girl and you aren't the hot girl! Why would they send you for this?'

Wait! I was confused. I was clearly hot enough for the old dude to hit on me in the hallway, but I wasn't hot enough to read a few measly lines for this irritable casting woman? Should I turn around and show her my arse? A mere five minutes before I'd been told it was fabulous. Perhaps the other casting guy was right, maybe I should get a boob job? In the end I didn't get the role, or any boob job. I just left with my tail between my legs and went out for a burger and a beer. Alone again because of the carbs.

It wasn't all bad, but LA definitely wasn't for me. I'm not cut out for that shit at all. In Australia, the auditioning scene is way less traumatic, as most of the major casting people are generally kind and encouraging. So I left LA and came home, where I thought I had a better chance of scoring a job and the casting people were nicer and never once mentioned my boobs.

◆

Returning home, I was fortunate enough to have a beautiful piece of work behind me that would hopefully open doors. Sometimes, however, I felt uncomfortable to be given so much positive attention on my first big job when I was only one part of the whole package. I hope that I shone a light on others – the writer, directors, cast members, all the people who made the magic happen – as much as they deserved. I'm not sure I did enough, but I was always fully aware of how rare and magical that experience had been. Without Josie I wonder if I would have stayed on *Neighbours*? Would I have gotten another lucky break, or transitioned to another career? I'm not sure, but I do think about it from time to time. Who would I be without Josie? Would life be better or worse? I don't know the answer to that question because she invaded my soul, changed my life and then we became one. Forever entwined.

Being an actor can definitely be fun, but it can also feel kind of absurd. Sometimes people ask me how I stayed grounded and I answer that a confusing mix of fame and poverty will do that to you. When *Alibrandi* was finally released, many of us were thrust into the spotlight in a way that was instantly life-changing. I'd always wondered what fame would be like, but when it happened, it happened so fast that it was hard to wrap my head around it. We *Alibrandi* alumni stuck together as a gang. For a while people would have extreme emotional reactions when they saw us, so it was better to share the experience with friends.

It was, however, an exciting time to be young, in a massive hit, doing press junkets and going to fancy events. People everywhere were so inviting and supportive. I was now living in Sydney where I didn't know many people, so I was making lots of new friends. As it goes with fame, some friendships lasted and some didn't, but the ones that did were fantastic.

In a lucky twist, the publicists I was working with at the film company were an excellent bunch of people and I made some great lifelong friends. One of my great loves was Tom, who used to pick me up in his old beaten-up Toyota Corolla and drive me around to all of my interviews and photo shoots. He was handsome and tall and skinny as a rake (mostly from anxiety, which made me love him more). We would laugh and laugh and make fun of everything, and somewhere along the journey he became my new wingman. He had just started dating a guy called Ant and before I knew it, I was a regular on their couch eating pizza and bingeing *Survivor*. We stayed friends and nothing much has changed really; more than twenty years later, our gang has just got bigger with our kids and my husband joining the group. To find a lasting, deep friendship in the middle of all this mayhem was a gift.

◆

The press tour for *Looking for Alibrandi* kicked on and even though the success was amazing and overwhelming, I was feeling a little bit in limbo. I'd managed to pick up some theatre work and some guest roles, but for the most part, I wasn't working much. I won an AFI award and had received beautiful reviews for *Alibrandi* (besides the one guy whose review in a major newspaper said I had a face like a cat's bum), but I was still green and trying to find my feet artistically. Having such a huge hit as my first big role was great because it could open doors, but I still felt like a work in progress and I wasn't landing many parts.

I really wanted to work. I'd had a taste of how fulfilling an amazing acting experience could be, and I was excited to see where it was going to take me. I was happy when I finally booked an ad. Not my dream job, but for the first time ever, I made good money. I probably should have squirrelled the cash away, but I was determined to study acting in New York. I'd been feeling unsure whether I had the technique to equal the quality of roles I was now auditioning for because I just didn't have the experience, and I found that I was getting way too nervous in auditions. I had to go back to the drawing board, develop the tools I needed to make my own way and then find my path. Ever since the *Alibrandi* bootcamps when I had worked with Nico Lathouris, whose method had been gritty and real and easy to digest, I had wanted to study practical aesthetics. I knew I should do it while I had the chance, so I decided to go to New York.

In the end, taking time off to study was the greatest decision I made. My experience at the Atlantic Theater Company in New York was challenging as well as fulfilling, and I felt myself start to settle into my own skin. I came back to Australia refreshed and clear-headed. I had finally learnt to stand on my own two feet as an actor with strength and gusto; I was given a new-found energy.

The next few years were filled with career peaks and troughs. I had many good jobs and lots of downtime in between, waiting for a call. This is completely normal in Australia – it's not uncommon to see brilliant actors working in bookshops or bars around Sydney. I too needed the financial security of a job, but the fame from *Alibrandi* stuck for a long time. I briefly wondered whether people would ever see past Josie. Eventually, I found voice-overs a good side hustle and I learnt to be versatile so, in time, I found a path that was the new normal. It took me a while to find my feet, but Josie was the reason I found love and had a family, so I could never have stayed mad at her for long.

CHAPTER NINETEEN

That's Amore

HARRY WARREN AND JACK BROOKS

The first time my husband saw me was on a popcorn box, and the way he tells it, his first thought was, 'I am going to marry her.' It sounds like some kind of psychic moment, but I just think it was because he likes Italian women. I like handsome, scruffy blond guys who play guitar, so we are literally a match made in heaven. He was in a band and we met when he asked his record company to approach me to appear in one of his film clips. He was stoked to meet the Italian girl from the popcorn box, I was stoked about the $1500 they were going to pay me to be in the clip.

I have already admitted I am not into romantic comedies and cheesy notions of love, but I have to admit that it was a pretty romantic meeting. I don't want to talk too much about my husband, Luke, because we are pretty private about our relationship – he has to share me a lot so we try to keep 'us' to ourselves. He works as a crew member on TV shows and as anyone who has been on a set knows, crew love to good-naturedly rib each other, so I can't put him through too much trauma by being soppy. And soppy isn't our jam. In saying all that, I have to give Luke his own chapter because we have pretty much grown up together.

When we met, both twenty-seven, I knew almost instantly that my fate was sealed. It was pretty hard not to fall in love with him, and so I did. It wasn't a giddy, out-of-control feeling but one of peace and relaxation because I had found my person. When I watched Luke perform I would melt a bit – he is a born entertainer with such presence and old-school rock star vibes. It took a while for things to warm up between us – despite that hot stage presence, he was actually very shy – but when things did take off we were all-in. A few weeks into our relationship, I had an epiphany when I looked at his hands and thought, *I'm going to grow old with these hands.* I guess we both had a psychic moment.

Luke and I were at the start of our careers with burgeoning success. We were healthily/unhealthily cynical about how everything worked in our respective industries and we'd shared as many highs as we had lows. So much heightened nonsense surrounds you when you are young in the entertainment industry and even though we were newbies, we were already feeling a bit depleted by all the fuss. We found each other in a similar space and we grounded each other. Once we had that, we didn't need all of the extra stuff, and together we retreated into our happy place, which was great for our souls, but possibly not so much for our careers. We didn't care though because to find a partner who is your best friend is truly a lucky break. We embarked on a journey together that was simple and easy.

Four months after we got together, we were married at the Graceland Wedding Chapel in Las Vegas by a guy with tattoos of love and hate on his knuckles. He was such a cool cat and it was pretty much my dream wedding. I saw a sign out the front that read: 'Lorenzo Lamas and Jon Bon Jovi got married here' and I looked at Luke and said excitedly, 'This is the place.' So that's where we got married. We had margaritas and nachos for dinner and ended the night sipping champagne in bed watching trashy TV – it was a Maury Povich talk show episode about a woman terrified of olives. Bliss. Our wedding rings cost us $22 from a cheap jeweller in Singapore and when I woke up I looked at the ring on my finger and thought, 'Well, that was a full-on thing to do.' We called our parents that morning and told them the news and although his mum and dad had never met me and were probably traumatised, they sweetly feigned enthusiasm and congratulated us. It turned out okay because I won them over.

That was the beginning of us and our long marriage together. We spent most of our time in Sydney just being together while he was writing a new record and I hung around waiting for the phone to ring. It was a pretty standard musician/actor vibe, without the drugs and money. We would hang out with Tom and Ant on weekends, watching *Survivor*, and go to the gym or take long walks to keep ourselves sane while we weren't busy. Luckily we never tired of each other's company because we were together a lot, and when our creative lives were often at a standstill most of our days were spent trying to keep ourselves occupied. I would occasionally head off to do a job and Luke eventually went away to record his new album, but for the most part we hung out in our little one-bedroom rental in Potts Point and ambled through our days. I would read books and he would sit in the bedroom writing songs, which sounds romantic and we knew it was, but we were always a bit stressed about the future, so that kept a lid on it a little.

We lived above a tiny cafe called Matchbox in Potts Point that was run by a sweet married couple. I loved the muesli cookies that they sold, so my favourite thing to do was to get up early and treat us to a coffee and a cookie. We would sit on the couch, chatting or watching morning *Will & Grace* reruns. I would dip that delicious cookie in my strong soy latte and savour every bite – it was the sweetest, most delicious treat. I still look for those cookies everywhere with their big chunks of dates and nuts and probably a mountain of sugar. In my early twenties when I was on *Neighbours*, I would start the day with a Caramello koala dipped in a Nescafé for breakfast (accompanied by the occasional Marlborough), so this was a definite step up in the nutrition stakes.

Now I'm older I understand why they make movies about young people in love meandering through their lives before kids and routine take over. It's the time of life that is filled with promise and anticipation, but it's also fraught with dull feelings of anxiety about what lies ahead. What does the future hold? Will everything be okay? What if something bad happens to me or someone I love? I started to get consumed by these thoughts all over again, and I couldn't shake the feeling that something terrible was about to happen. I was also dealing with a strange medical issue and it had triggered so much anxiety in me that it was stopping me from really being able to enjoy life.

◆

Just before I met Luke (around the time *Alibrandi* was released), I was recovering from a bad flu when my eye began to twitch. It twitched for a week, then my lip started to twitch, then my tongue, then my fingers and toes and thighs, progressively getting worse. They weren't violent spasms, just small muscle twitches that would go off all over my body incessantly. It was exhausting. Underneath my feet felt like ants were running through my veins and these strange pins and needles would make it hard to fall asleep. My muscles would get tired and I had a weird sense of detachment from the left side of my body that made it hard to lift anything to my mouth, so I made sure I only used my right hand when I held anything. I visited doctor after doctor and was told that I was tired and it would go away, but it didn't, it just got worse.

I was in Adelaide doing a theatre production of Ibsen's *The Wild Duck* and while I was enjoying the work and trying to be present, I couldn't shake these twitches. The late nights in the theatre made them worse. I went to an internet cafe one day and googled 'involuntary muscle twitches', and symptoms for ALS and MS came up on the screen. I panicked so I took myself to emergency at the local hospital, but they sent me away and told me I was tired. I knew it was more than that. I rang my mum crying and begged for help in that way you do when things are really scary and only your mum can rescue you. Mum has always worked for doctors so I was hoping she would know someone or something. She eventually found a doctor for me and I made an appointment for when I got back to Sydney.

Dr Rob worked in a medical practice in Darlinghurst; he was young, cool and kind. His specialty was sexual health and he dealt with a lot of vulnerable people in the LGBTQIA+ community who were struggling with mental and physical issues. I could tell he was special. I liked him immediately – he was the first person who really listened to me about my bizarre symptoms without being dismissive. My anxiety by then was crippling and my health issues were freaking me out. He said that I needed to see a neurologist, then he booked me into the anxiety clinic at St Vincent's Hospital for a twelve-month program. I felt so relieved to have someone in my corner.

Luke took me to my appointments with the neurologist so that I never felt alone and afraid. My neuro exam results were always passable (it's a long physical evaluation), but after the nerve conduction tests the doctor could tell my nerves were damaged. He said it could perhaps be MS or something worse, but I had to wait three months to undertake more nerve conduction tests to see if the nerves had healed or if the damage was more extensive.

During those three months of waiting, I alternated between fearing the worst and hoping for the best. Whenever I warned Luke about what might be coming for me physically, he said he didn't care how hard it got because he would always stick by me. I knew he was telling me the truth. I was right, too, because he always has.

Living with me through those months of dark thoughts can't have been easy, but he did a good job of helping me keep things in perspective. I've always had a penchant for health worries and Luke is someone who will avoid the doctor until he is at death's door. Our polar opposite attitudes actually complement each other in times of crisis.

When I finally returned to the neurologist for the follow-up nerve conduction tests, he found I had improved a little, which was good news. He couldn't rule out MS completely, but it wasn't a terrible result and I was grateful for that.

For the next five years I needed to continue seeing the neurologist regularly. Things stayed the same and the twitches have continued. In fact, I'm sitting in bed right now twitching away with pins and needles in my feet, but I'm used to it. The neurologist eventually told me it was likely I had something called benign fasciculation syndrome, which is twitches that occur without any underlying medical condition. But this syndrome doesn't usually cause nerve damage, so he couldn't rule out something more sinister. He was confident I was remaining stable, however, so I just got on with life.

I showed Luke this story and I think he may have thought that banging on about twitches was a bit out of place in a chapter about us, but it makes sense to me because at no point was I worried that he would check out if things got hard.

That's a story worth telling. I had a friend who died of breast cancer around the same time, so this whole experience taught me that growing older is a privilege that some people don't get to enjoy. Whenever I feel crummy about my twitches, my wrinkles or my perimenopause (not fun), I think about what could have been and I feel appreciative.

◆

Twitching aside, life rolled on, as it does. We both weathered career ups and downs, supporting each other through it all. Lucky for me I have a group of supportive friends as well. Actors are great at rallying around each other when times are tough – laughing through awful auditions or rehashing bad experiences together while drinking tea and eating chips. Occasionally, for really awful times, we might swig a whiskey or three and order pizza. Musicians don't always have that supportive community; well, Luke didn't, and so when he struggled I think he had nowhere to turn, which is why his focus on his music career faded away. But it wasn't just his doing.

The music industry wasn't a great place for everyone, and this was particularly problematic for a shy boy from Queensland. Publicly, the band appeared to be doing quite well, but behind the scenes it was a crushing experience for Luke because not all artists are equipped to deal with the machinations of their chosen industry. It is sad to think of the amazing talent that may have stepped away from the spotlight because too often it wasn't about the music, but personalities and power. The music oligarchy have recently had their comeuppance, but at the time they were all-powerful and held the fate of an artist's future in their hands, ready to squeeze the life out of anyone who wouldn't compromise their values. Toeing the line was hard because it also meant drugs, sex, parties, and that's not the path everyone wants to take to succeed. It certainly wasn't my husband's. It's not my story to tell, but I think it's important to remember that when an industry has so many toxic elements and is so powerful, it's often the gentle souls who get destroyed. Luke eventually turned his back on the industry and his musical career. The trauma of it all was an uninvited third wheel in our relationship for a long time. It sort of still is. Although he did his best to shut the door on it, he never quite could. His story was painful and even though at his core he is still a brilliant musician who I admire, he couldn't move past his negative experience. Instead, he has chosen to spend his time writing and recording beautiful songs that stay in our garage, because that's where they are safe.

Lots of artists have their stories of pain and many have their stories of joy. For us it's a mix of both, although I have been lucky to have had more joy than pain in my career, and I'm so grateful for that. Whatever happens in our journey it's been nice to hold each other's hands through it all. That's important when you don't have a regular job because your self-esteem can take hits from all the rejection. To come home to someone who thinks you are amazing is a lucky break. We may not have scaled the heights that we dreamt of as little kids, but we did okay; in some ways, we did better, because life became more important than career, and that's nothing to bellyache about.

◆

Around this time, in the early 2000s, we moved to the mountains to get some peace and air. We'd hit our 30s and thought a change of pace might be nice. Luke loved it, but I was a bit unhappy, cold and damp, and the phone service was shit. I watched way too much *Ready, Steady, Cook* and there are only so many pies I could bake or bushwalks I could take. I'm a city mouse who likes the beach, not the mountains. To cheer me up, Luke got me a dog. I'd had Toto from *Wizard of Oz* fantasies my whole life and had been talking incessantly for years about getting a Toto of my own. I called him Tuffy. My beautiful boy. The day I met Tuffy he was at the back of the pack staring at me while his brothers and sisters clambered all over me, full of confidence and energy. He was trying to get to me, but he couldn't because he lacked a bit of confidence – I knew he was for me.

We were inseparable from the moment I held Tuffy in my arms. He was a beautiful little Australian Silky Terrier that was a perfect combination of anxious and kooky, and we spent every moment together, completely obsessed with each other. After only a year in the mountains, Luke and I moved back to the city, to cafe life and good phone service. I felt bad because he'd loved it there, but I was feeling so heavy. I think the city was initially a bit loud for Tuffy, although he eventually got used to it. He loved me so much he would wee in my suitcase every time I packed to go away for work, and when I returned home he would refuse to look at me for a day or two just to punish me for leaving him. Not everyone was a fan – he loved to hump my friends (especially the ladies), but he was so cute it was hard to stay annoyed with him. I took him everywhere with me. I helped him through his anxieties and he helped me through mine. And when they say a dog is good training for babies, they aren't wrong.

With Tuffy by our side, life moved on and it seemed to be going fast. Luke began a regular job while he still tinkered with music and I would do voice-overs for money while I looked for acting work. If I managed to book one or two acting jobs a year that would make me happy because I love being on set. We paved out a quiet little life for ourselves. And through it all we had our routine of watching *Survivor* with Tom and Ant on weekends. Eventually, I heard my babies calling me so we began planning the next chapter of our lives. As it is with babies, that's when things started to go fast and slow at the same time.

CHAPTER TWENTY

No matter where you go or turn,
you will always end up at home.

ITALIAN SAYING

I was surprised by how stressful trying to fall pregnant was. One minute I was young and free and then in the blink of an eye I was told that I was past my 'peak fertile years', which made the fear set in, but also annoyed me. I know there are medical realities to age and fertility, but at thirty-five I still felt full of life, so to hear the message that my ovaries were possibly past their prime was frustrating. It's not that simple having kids when you work in the arts, which I think is why a lot of us put it off. There is no maternity leave or job security and there aren't many acting jobs for pregnant women, so the prospect of not working or earning for a year was daunting. On top of that, to get the not-so-subtle message that I was on the slide, well, isn't that nice.

I always wanted to be a mother and dreamt of having two girls who would be close and go through life as a team like Nicole and I have. I love having a sister, even though we used to fight a lot when we were young and occasionally hurled pieces of fruit at each other. I feel so lucky to have that relationship and I can't imagine not having her there. I see a lot of Nicole and me in her two boys, in their relationship, their differences and similarities. Watching them grow up together from boisterous little boys into young men has been a privilege, and I wanted to add to our family and experience motherhood for myself.

I might have been ready for motherhood, but getting pregnant took longer than I thought. It was a strange feeling because I'd spent most of my adult life trying *not* to get pregnant. I started wondering if maybe it just wasn't a possibility and as much fun as it is for the husbands, I think it also gets a bit tiring. Sometimes I would look at my period tracker and be like 'NOW! We have to do it . . . NOW!' Then, after about ten months of harassing my husband and hoping to see two lines appear on a pregnancy test, I finally fell pregnant.

As a semi-professional hypochondriac I was surprised by how relaxed I was during the pregnancy. For all my bitching and moaning about not being able to work as a pregnant woman I actually managed to shoot a film in my second trimester, which was tiring but wonderful because it was completely unexpected. There are lots of amusing scenes with me holding bags and vases in front of my stomach to cover my growing belly, but for the most part it went fairly smoothly. My morning (all day) sickness had passed and aside from complete exhaustion, it was nice to have some distraction and be around creative people every day.

I did manage to vomit into the bin of every Coles and Woolworths supermarket I passed through. Sometimes also in an IGA. I am still not sure why supermarkets triggered an attack but they did, every time.

Once filming was over I was ready to lie down for a few weeks. Everyone kept advising me to get as much sleep as I could because I wouldn't be getting any at all soon enough. It was summer by this stage and we had no air-conditioning in our old townhouse so sleeping was tricky. I knew I was having a girl by this stage so all the discomfort mattered little because my mind was blown with happiness. I spent the last couple of months with my swollen feet in a bucket of baking soda eating Cheese Twisties, Frosty Fruits and watching reruns of *Survivor* with Tuffy by my side.

I was nervous about labour so I chose to work with the midwives at the birth centre at Royal Prince Alfred Hospital in inner Sydney, knowing that if anything went wrong they could rush me into the hospital for medical help. It felt like a good compromise between my desire to be a chilled earth mother and my crippling fear that something could go wrong. The day I went into labour I woke up at 4 a.m. with an excruciating pain in my back; it happened again thirty minutes later and then again, so by 6 a.m. I knew for sure that I was in labour. I was a bit confused because I thought the pain would be in my stomach and not my back. I called my sister at 6.30 a.m. and the first thing she said was, 'Are you in labour because I woke up at 4 a.m. and felt like you were, and I have been lying here waiting for you to call me.' Sisters know.

Luke found it very hard to get me to go to hospital because I thought that if I stayed at home then I could delay what I knew was going to be an unimaginably painful event. Tom came over to get Tuffy and I think he was a bit shocked by the fact I was pretending everything was normal, offering him tea, then rolling around on the floor screaming in pain, then jumping up to offer him a biscuit. It was next-level denial. Luke got the midwives on the phone, who firmly told me that I had to come to hospital immediately, so I did. It turned out the baby was posterior and a posterior natural birth is less than fun, but we made it through, after hours of torture. The midwife promised me I would have a baby by the time *Bold and the Beautiful* started at 4.30 p.m. I was keen to watch it because there was something big going on with Brooke and Ridge, so I kept pushing, hoping to make my soapie deadline. She was right. I had a beautiful baby girl at 3.58 p.m. I missed the episode though, because

I couldn't stop staring at her. I looked into this little person's eyes and I was changed forever. I told her, 'This is the beginning of a big adventure together, I hope I make you proud.' We called her Lily. My Lily.

◆

I'd been to all of the antenatal classes and read all of the books, but nothing can really prepare you for the unpredictability and loneliness of new motherhood. Nothing is in your control and sometimes the people who try to help can, unintentionally, make things worse because your head and hormones are all over the place. The hospital sent me home with a massive booklet about breastfeeding that was filled with stories of engorged breasts, leaks and oversupply so I was anxiously awaiting for my bosoms to erupt like Mount Etna. They never did. It was before the internet was as proficient as it is today, so I pored through the booklet, looking for some help. There was nothing. Not one sentence about a starving baby and low milk supply, not a word in this massive tome, so I quietly decided that I was a freak and a failure and fell into an emotional hole. Midwives suggested I avoid formula to keep my baby hungry so that she would continue sucking as a survival instinct. I always imagined myself as someone who would have a baby latched to my breast all day, but instead my milk would run out by 4 p.m. and no amount of pumping would help.

Mothers' group was a disaster. I would turn up frazzled and embarrassed while some of the mums would look at me pityingly and say, 'Well, your body knows what to do, you just need to persist.' Persist? I was pumping day and night and following all of the advice to try to give my baby my milk, because back then breastfeeding was a hot topic and using formula gave me a white-hot shame. Eventually, when Lily lost too much weight, I began topping her up, while continuing to pump and feed her as much breastmilk as I could. A friend, who had the same issue, warned me, 'You can't do a formula feed in public or people will stare and sometimes tell you off, so you just have to arrange outings outside feeding times.' I was so deep in my shame I didn't realise how messed up it all was.

I think attitudes have changed now, but it's good to remember that sometimes the pressure on new mothers is bullshit. You are so vulnerable when you are a first-time parent and there is this pressure to follow a certain path. When that path isn't available to you, feelings of failure can set in; well, they did for me. Some people reading this might still say, 'Well, she mustn't have tried hard enough,' but let me tell you, I did – many of us do and still don't succeed – so kindly jog on.

Living so far away from Nicole and Mum, who were both in Melbourne, Luke and I decided to make the move to Victoria. We relocated just in time for me to have my second baby. My Jimmy. I'd had a miscarriage just before I fell pregnant with him so I wasn't as relaxed in my pregnancy as I had been with Lily. I would run to the bathroom incessantly in the first trimester looking for signs that I was going to lose him, but I didn't. Although I was pretty unwell through this pregnancy, I was ecstatic to be having baby number two.

I was a little shocked to find I wouldn't have two girls, but when Jimmy arrived and I looked into his blue eyes, I knew he was the perfect match for Lily. I could tell he had the sweetest soul.

I was much kinder to myself on this second journey and the midwives at the Freemasons' feeding clinic had a more holistic approach, so we found a feeding routine that worked for us without pressure and judgement. Although I still managed to judge myself, just a bit.

Despite being in my hometown with Nicole and Mum closer, I still felt isolated. My friends didn't live close by, Luke was working a lot and so I spent my days alone with my babies. We passed the time dancing to the *Frozen* soundtrack and going for long walks with Tuffy. I watched *Frozen* so many times that I actually started to find Kristoff the reindeer guy hot, a detail that Lily will never let me forget. I do stand by the fact that he seems nice, though.

When I was really lonely, I would drag the kids into the Italian grocer just so I could have a chat to the ladies behind the deli. One of the perks of being Josie Alibrandi is that Italians are usually up for a chat and when you go to the deli it's not unusual to get a few slices of free prosciutto or mortadella. It's a wonderful perk I could not have predicted.

◆

My kids loved to tantrum all over town: long, loud tantrums that no-one could miss. On these days I wished I was invisible. People often seemed to recognise me when my child was crying or when I was feeling tired and vulnerable. I knew that part of the responsibility of being Josie Alibrandi was to make peoples' day, but when you look like shit after a day of wrangling toddlers and babies, sometimes you just want to hide.

When you are recognised but not so known that people feel you are off-limits, interactions can be tricky and not always pleasant. I don't mind the incessant *Alibrandi* jokes, 'Hey, we found her', or 'Stop looking for Alibrandi, she's here!' I actually love it. I also like how people think I've never heard it before. I enjoy giving them the thrill of thinking they invented it. It's cute.

But there've been moments when I've been pounced on while looking my worst, feeling sad or facing a 15–0 strikeout after auditions for jobs. On those days, it's harder to shrug off comments like, 'Oh, I remember you, what happened to you?' or 'Must be hard being an actor, ever thought about going to Hollywood? Guess it's a bit late now.' And 'That Nicole Kidman has a good career. Have you ever thought of doing that?' Or 'Gosh, I almost didn't recognise you, you are so much older!' *Yep, yep, thank you* . . . keep smiling, always smiling. But feel free to slowly die inside.

After a couple of years of juggling pregnancies and not having much work I was lucky to pick up some lovely jobs while Lily was a toddler and James was a baby. I worked on great Aussie dramas like *The Time of Our Lives* and *Wentworth*, so when people in the street asked me what happened to my career I could excitedly say, 'I'm working, I just did a job!' But really I was thinking, 'I'm more than Josie, praise Jesus I'm more than Josie.'

It was confusing because I felt like I no longer had ownership of myself after *Alibrandi*. And the exhaustion of motherhood made it more complicated. The irony of losing my identity after making a film about a girl searching for hers is not lost on me.

◆

What happened? All those sleepless nights and then my thirties were gone in a flash. Luke was working long hours in television to make ends meet and I was home with the kids, waiting for the phone to ring. Jobs popped up occasionally, which I was always grateful for, and I was starting to land more comedy roles, which had always been my happy place. The truth is for most Australian actors, even in a good year you could have six to eight months of unemployment. It is a tough industry and as you get older and accumulate more responsibilities it feels even harder. Once the kids started to get older I was determined to somehow turn things around for my family, but I just wasn't sure how.

I knew how lucky we were. We had a roof over our heads, two wonderful children and we both had our health. For the most part we were happy because that's really all we needed. The kids had loving parents and grandparents. We would sometimes drive up to Queensland to see Luke's parents and they would dote on Lily and Jimmy in that cosy old-school way that grandparents do. The kids had family around and as they grew up they collected some lovely friends. Tuffy was with us every minute and he would bedhop between us all at night. The kids had slumber parties and went on camp and we tried to spoil them at Christmas. Ours was a sweet and standard suburban life. Luke and I were sometimes stressed and tired, but looking back I can see that we were mostly content in our little cocoon, even though daily pressures sometimes clouded that. We didn't need much although we often dreamt of more, but my forties had crept up on me and it seemed our lives were now set in stone. It wasn't bad, it was good, but I always had this weird tingly feeling that something else was on the horizon. I was right about that. It just wasn't what any of us expected.

CHAPTER TWENTY-ONE

If I would ever pass you along in life again and you were
laying there dying of thirst, I would not give you a drink
of water. I would let the vultures take you and do what-
ever they want with ya, with no ill regrets. I plead to the
jury tonight to think a little bit about the island that we
have been on. This island is full of pretty much only two
things: snakes and rats. And in the end of Mother Nature,
we have Richard the snake, who knowingly went after prey,
and Kelly, who turned into the rat, that ran around like
the rats do on this island, trying to run from the snake.
I feel we owe it to the island's spirits, that we have learned
to come to know, to let it be in the end the way Mother
Nature intended it to be, for the snake to eat the rat.

SUSAN HAWK, *SURVIVOR: BORNEO*

My toxic trait is that I know this speech by heart.

I fell in love with *Survivor* hard. The first season
completely blew my mind. It was so good! It was raw and

epic and I had never seen anything like that before on television. It quickly became my favourite show, but it was the game of *Survivor* itself that really got me excited. The first season appeared before reality TV contestants were savvy and performed for the camera or were vying for Instagram followers. It was just people playing a game to the death and I was obsessed.

Watching Richard Hatch and Kelly Wiglesworth hash it out at that first final tribal gave me butterflies. I fantasised about sitting there. I loved how Richard nailed it and I also obsessed over how Kelly could have argued her case to take the crown. Sue's speech at the end was so catastrophically mind-blowing and then Gervase Peterson's clapback to her when he cast his final vote was the icing on the cake. If you haven't seen it I recommend watching it – it has this incredible retro vibe because the contestants are cutting their teeth in a game and genre that was so new and unknown.

This is going to sound bonkers to non-*Survivor*-type people, but for some of us, *Survivor* runs in our blood. I'm not sure why. Many people can watch *Survivor* and enjoy it as a TV show, but for me it was something that I instantly started to obsess over. From the year 2000, I was completely distracted by a compelling desire to go and play that game. I never missed a season and even though I was also obsessed with *The Sopranos*, *Survivor* was the show I dreamt of being cast in. Also, that possibility seemed more realistic.

A few years in, I decided that it would be a brilliant idea to apply for the US version (it was the only version at that time). I don't like the bush or bugs or too much nature or camping or being dirty. But I do like the beach and I don't tend to burn in the sun, so I figured that was something. The main reason I wanted to apply was that I was completely fixated on winning. Also Tom and I thought Jeff Probst was hot. I looked online and to my dismay I found out that you needed to be an American citizen to play. Bummer.

Luke and I joked that we could divorce, then I could quickly put together a marriage of convenience with an American friend, come home after a win on *Survivor*, divorce my friend, marry each other again and spend my million dollars. It was all good fun, but I was still slightly miffed that I would never get a chance to play. I did feel like I would be an easy first vote out with my spaghetti arms, bad swimming technique and fear of heights, so I reassured myself that it was probably a good thing and I was saved from public humiliation.

I was a bit irritating to watch *Survivor* with. Thank God everyone seemed to enjoy my incessant ranting about who should stick together and who should've done what and why.

Analysing the tactics is part of the fun and that's what the show is about – audience participation from the comfort of your couch with a bowl of ice cream while watching people starve and suffer.

Luke, God bless him, used to really take in what I was saying and tell me that he didn't understand how my brain could keep up with all of the alliances and nuances of tribal life. I think I was able to do it not because I was a genius strategist, but because I always imagined myself there and I loved the relationship side of it. Sometimes I would groan aloud at the end of tribal council and say, 'I told you!' Then I would smugly whisper to my glass of wine, 'If I wasn't first out, I could so win this.' Tom and I would fantasise about competing in a family visit challenge together – we promised each other we'd throw it because winning the family reward is a death knell. Fans will get this . . . its equivalent to the car curse. We were mentally prepared, just in case.

When we moved to Melbourne I missed my *Survivor* nights with Ant and Tom. Whenever I was in Sydney we would try to watch it together, just like old times. As the years went on my obsession waxed and waned, but it was always there in the background, a loyal friend and a comfort – everything I love about great television.

◆

In 2018 I had been shooting a wonderful kids TV show called *Mustangs FC*. I absolutely loved being a part of something so positive and new. I was asked to do an interview to promote it with a great TV blog called 'TV Tonight', so I happily bashed out a written Q and A for a segment called 'What I've been watching' early on New Year's Day, 2019. Part of it read like this:

Which guilty pleasure show are you reluctant to admit to watching?

PM: Well . . . I know actors aren't meant to like reality but I'm a massive Survivor *fan. I never miss a season. I'm having so much fun watching Mike White on the current US season that I'm squealing at the television! I also loved the last season of* Australian Survivor, *I thought it was so great.*

What show would you secretly love to appear on?

PM: Well obviously Survivor *but I'm not sure I could go that long without a bowl of pasta and a set of tweezers. Also if I didn't make the jury I would be DEVASTATED! I'd never get over it.*

When I first answered the question about what show I would love to appear on, I initially wrote something highbrow and impressive. Since it was New Year's I stopped myself, erased my answer and wrote *Survivor* because, truthfully, when I watched *Australian Survivor* I was annoyed that I wasn't on it. I wasn't intending to try to get on the show, I was just having a New Year moment. I showed Luke my answers so he could proofread them (which I often do) and, looking at my *Survivor* response, he said, 'Geez P, be careful what you wish for.' I laughed at him, 'Oh my God, no-one is asking me to go on *Survivor*, that would never happen!'

Well, I was wrong because on Monday morning, 7 January 2019, my agents received an email.

> Hi Guys,
> I hope you enjoyed your Christmas and New Year break.
> I wanted to have a chat with Pia's agent re the below article.
>
> https://tvtonight.com.au/2018/12/what-ive-been-watching-pia-miranda.html
>
> I am currently casting the 'Champions' team for Survivor 2019 and would love to talk to her about her interest and availability, especially as she has mentioned in the article how much she would love to appear on the show.
>   Could the best person give me a call on the below mobile number so we can chat further about the details of the opportunity? In the meantime have a look at the attached presentation and note we won the AACTA award for 'Best Reality Program' last year.
>
> Looking forward to hearing your thoughts.

Oh shit!

◆

Even after all my years of obsessing about the show, my first response was that I didn't want to do it, I really didn't . . . but also, I couldn't stop thinking about it.

I'd been deep in mum and work life for so many years that I hadn't even thought that something like this might be possible. Raising kids can mute your ambition, which isn't always a bad thing, but it meant that when this opportunity came along, it felt like an alien concept. I love being home with young kids, I really do. I cherish that feeling of waking up in the morning and having nothing else to do other than hang out with my babies, but I'm sure lots of parents will agree that during the process of raising kids you also lose a bit of yourself. I think that's probably how nature intended it, so that we realise it's no longer 'our time' and that we must pass the baton of life off to the younger generation. But then they went off to school and I had my days free again which gave me that weird 'What next?' feeling. Maybe I should play *Survivor*?

I walked around with a knot in my stomach. It was still a bit unusual at that time for actors to be on reality TV and I worried how it would be perceived. But then I thought, 'Fuck what people think.' I turned to my agent, Tash, who has also been my friend for over twenty years, and asked for her opinion. Her response was, 'C'mon, at our age what do we have to lose? I think you should just take a risk!'

I knew she was right but I was so scared. They told me it was filming in Savusavu, Fiji, and there was a tiny light plane trip I would have to take to get out there so that was an immediate red flag. Plus fifty days on a remote island with minimal food and shelter and no contact with my family. Bugs, heights, ocean swimming, no pasta, possibly growing a moustache on television . . . so many intense fears. I'm also allergic to bees, so I obsessively googled, 'Are there lots of bees in Fiji?' *Oh my God,* I thought, *I can't win* Survivor, *I'm a massive wuss.*

I think any parent who goes to play *Survivor* has to wrestle with the guilt of leaving their family. You feel so irresponsible, but also in the back of your mind is that nagging thought – 'What if I could win?' While I was worrying about abandoning Luke and the kids, he was adamant that I should do it. I like to think because he knew I could win. Luke told me, 'You never take risks or do anything for yourself anymore. Go out and have an adventure and I'll hold the fort.' He loved *Survivor* too, but the reality of me leaving to take part in it seemed over-whelming, so we sat down and made a plan.

We worked out the cost and talked to people about helping out with the kids. When we decided we could do it, I made a promise that if I was going to leave my family for fifty days, I was going to play to win. Screw everything: if I was going to play *Survivor*, I was going to come back with the title no matter what.

◆

I began training straight away and, looking back now, there is quite a list of things that I did right. But there were also things I did wrong. And that list is quite substantial. Now, you would think as a superfan I would be across everything but, no, I was so obsessed with winning that I forgot to research a few important details. So for any future players here is my list of successes and failures.

Things I did right:
- Practised fire-making with flint.
- Did lots of yoga.
- Hired a high-performance coach (thanks, Tommy) to help me conquer my fear of heights by jumping off a high diving board. (*Australian Survivor* loves making people jump off high stuff.)
- Obsessively googled 'How to win *Survivor*'.
- Studied Sandra Diaz–Twine's strategy for winning twice and read every interview she had ever done. Thanks Sandra – 'Anyone but me' was my motto.
- Rewatched both Cochran seasons, because he blew his first time and nailed his second in such a dramatic way

that it is a masterclass in pivoting. (Worth a watch if you are ever going to play, but also worth a watch anyway because they are two great seasons.)

- Tried to learn how to swim freestyle properly. I did lots of early-morning laps.
- Ate copious amounts of pasta, burgers, chocolate and beer to bulk gain three weeks before heading in.
- Read up on what makes an annoying tribemate. I read that singing at camp was a sure-fire way to get voted out, so even though I wanted to sing show tunes all day on the beach out of boredom, I kept quiet.
- Learnt how to tweeze facial hair with seashells. Was originally for my own moustache, but in the end I had quite the beauty salon going out there.

Things I did wrong:
- Not enough weight training (apparently arm muscles are very important). My muppet arms failed me.
- Didn't research what to pack and instead obsessed about packing to look cute. None of my clothes were quick-drying fabrics so I was damp most of the time. Janine Allis, however, nailed the perfect packing brief. All future *Survivor* players should refer to her. Apparently merino wool is the key.
- After the producers changed my first-day outfit, I switched my leggings to jeans, forgetting that meant I

had no comfy pants to sleep in. We were permitted five extra items and mine were just tops and underwear. I probably should have worked that out. In the end I strategically stole clothes off the line from eliminated contestants after they were gone. Sorry, not sorry.

- Didn't learn to wrestle. *Australian Survivor* reward challenges are all about wrestling each other for food.
- Didn't learn how to throw and catch a ball. The fact that I can't even catch car keys should have been a red flag.
- Didn't prepare funny things to say when voting people out. Instead I tried to appear sweet to counteract the evil thoughts I had, so I just seem boring and possibly creepy.
- Didn't learn how to duck dive . . . still not really sure what that is. Thanks, Ross, for dragging me into the abyss more than once.
- Didn't google Fiji weather in May and June. I shouldn't have just assumed it would be hot. It wasn't.
- Didn't smuggle some moustache wax in my undies.

Anyway, before I knew it, it was time to leave. The family was organised so by the time I left I was feeling fairly ready, although I was still hoping to book an acting gig so that I didn't have to go. That may sound contradictory given all the years I'd spent wanting to be part of this game, but I was scared and I knew how much I was going to miss my family. Unfortunately, no gig came.

The worst part was that the day before I left, my daughter changed her mind about me going. I had asked Lily's and Jimmy's permission before I said yes and they were on board because they had grown up watching the show. As the reality of it kicked in, Lily panicked and didn't want me to leave. She was so little, only nine, and I realised it was a lot to have her mum go away for seven weeks. But it was too late. I felt my heart smash into a million pieces as I held her in my arms on her bedroom floor and she begged, 'Please act horrible so they vote you out first!' I said I would try as guilt and panic washed over me and I realised I didn't want to go and leave my beautiful family. I grabbed her face and looked into her eyes and said, 'If I win, I promise I will take you to Disneyland, okay?' Lily wasn't having any of it; she said she didn't want Disneyland, she only wanted me. My heart smashed even more. I tried to stay positive and thought that if I could get through this and take my baby on her first big holiday, it might all just be worth it.

Fifty days is a long time and I felt sick with fear – I didn't think I could do it. Somehow I summoned up the courage to say goodbye to my family at the airport and I walked through the departure gate, alone and scared. If I was going to cause them all this pain, I had better go and win it.

I spotted two of my potential tribemates in the airport lounge and I sized them up. I wasn't sure who they were. Even though we had a minder and weren't allowed to talk, I tried to look innocent and smiled at them sweetly. The game had just begun.

CHAPTER TWENTY-TWO

I came, I saw, I conquered.

JULIUS CAESAR

Spoiler alert.

I fucking won *Survivor*.

I wake up every morning and think to myself: *I. Fucking. Won*. Survivor.

It is incredible. I will never get over it.

Unfortunately for me, I didn't bounce back afterwards like I thought I would. Some people do, some don't. Many former players come out with the most positive, life-changing lessons, but a lot of us are also scarred in some way. On *Survivor: Winners at War*, competitor Tyson Apostol said, 'Some mentalities can handle it and some can't. It can ruin people's lives to lose the game. There's a lot of people that go home and struggle with it for years. For real.' I get that. I really do. I feel it. And I won.

The aftermath aside, it is still unbelievable to me that I got to play the game that I had loved obsessively for over twenty years. The absolute privilege and thrill of playing *Survivor* will never be lost on me and to know I will go to my grave with an unsnuffed torch and the title of Sole Survivor is a dream come true. Sometimes Tom will randomly say to me, 'You won *Survivor!*' and we both have a moment, because it means that much to us.

When I arrived in Savusavu after the world's hairiest plane trip I was quickly sequestered alone in a basic hotel room with a comically noisy ceiling fan and a tiny plunge pool filled with bugs. I enjoyed it – it was breezy and tropical and it had a cosy bed that I knew would be my last soft surface for a while. There was no TV, phone or internet so I did yoga, read a few books and ate as many of the snacks as I could. But my stomach was in knots, so it was hard to digest anything. The massive packet of chicken chips went down a treat though. Even at the worst of times, chicken chips have been there for me. (To a lesser degree, so have barbeque.)

Waiting in that room to go and play *Survivor* was like waiting to give birth, except I only had a one in twenty-four chance of bringing home a baby, and the baby was half a million dollars. I wanted it to hurry up and start, but I was also terrified of what was to come. A part of me wanted to run . . . but I couldn't because they already had my passport. Plus I really wanted the title.

Finally D-day arrived. Looking back, it's a bit of a blur. All I remember was being taken to a beach in a bus and when I got out they patted me down looking for contraband. I had heard a rumour a contestant once smuggled in a vial of cannabis oil in their butt. (Not saying who this was, but this contestant did seem pretty chill for the first half of the game until it was obviously confiscated at the three-quarter mark.) After playing, I totally get it, no judgement here. It actually would have been helpful.

The first thing that happened was I was told to go stand on the mat with my new tribe. I remember that the sun was blazing hot and my eyes were already stinging from the glare. I began to wonder how I was going to survive without sunglasses. I didn't know that was the least of my worries. I was trying to look calm and cool, but I felt instantly awkward in my body and suddenly I regretted my trying-too-hard boho outfit. My jeans were already sticky and uncomfortable and I began panicking about how I was going to sleep in them, which was a fair concern. I looked at my tribe and I instantly knew that I wasn't going to fit in because I recognised quite a few of them as retired athletes who already seemed to have a rapport. I had no clue as to how I was going to mentally or physically cope with it all,

I wanted to cry and I was already homesick. After scoping out my tribe, winning suddenly seemed very unlikely.

I was the smallest and definitely the weakest. *Australian Survivor* values brute strength in the pre-merge game more than its US counterpart, and I could already feel a target being burnt onto my back. To add insult to injury, the first competition was a wrestling challenge and I knew I was going to be a complete disaster. I think I was secretly hoping for a dance-off.

Everyone was being paired up in one-on-one wrestling matches and I was thinking about how I would strategically survive this first hurdle. My tribe was dripping in alpha male sweat and bravado. They seemed very grunty and I tried to fit in by screaming out some overly enthusiastic 'yeahhhhh's when my teammates pummelled an opponent into the ground. I knew I wasn't quite pulling it off, but I did my best. I chose the tallest and strongest lady from the other tribe to be my wrestling partner because I thought, 'Well at least when I fail I can blame the uneven match-up.' Good strategy. It kind of worked and it kind of didn't.

When we got back to camp I scanned the group for potential friends and I naturally gravitated toward the women. I recognised Janine Allis pretty quickly, because I am very fond of a Boost Juice (that comment is not sponsored) and I always thought she was very glamorous on *Shark Tank*. I decided to try to bond with her and some of the other females as we weaved palm fronds together, which I unfortunately sucked at too.

We all pitched in to help with the shelter and even though I was personally working on the *Survivor* version of the Penske file, I tried to look busy so as not to expose my general uselessness in the outdoors. After a long day of awkward banter and walking around in circles, trying to look chill, the sun suddenly started to fall in the sky and the anxiousness of surviving the night immediately overwhelmed me. There was good reason for me to be nervous; that first night in camp was absolute torture. I was the coldest I've ever been. The men had been huffing and puffing all day making the shelter, but the floor was a disaster so a group of us just rolled around on the beach, moaning and complaining, until dawn. Janine and Abbey Holmes slept like babies in the shelter and I was immediately envious of their resilience. I think I caught an hour of sleep curled up by the fire, but it was definitely not a fun night and I worried about how I was going to get through another one.

The next day I started to chat with people a bit more easily, but the athletes seemed to already know each other and they appeared to have control of the tribe. I very obviously didn't fit in with them so I tried to be low-key, cheerful and help a lot around camp. That's all I had in my arsenal because absolutely no-one wanted to talk strategy with me and I knew that if they weren't talking to me, then they were talking about me. Not good.

I was used to a drama camp vibe where we would sit around, sing show tunes and tell stories about how we were a disappointment to our parents. Successful professional athletes were anything but because they liked to sit around and talk about their achievements. They seemed nice, but it was a bit like talking to aliens.

There were a few people who I was getting along well with, but even though I was pretty fit, I was obviously the weakest physically and the fact that I had never played a sport in my life was clearly a disadvantage. I felt like such an outsider. I could tell two of the guys found me borderline offensive, with my lack of physical strength and penchant for cracking self-deprecating jokes, but I was trying to distract them with some superficial charm, which was having only moderate to weak success.

Unfortunately we lost the first immunity challenge and I knew the tribe was coming for me. It wasn't really a secret. I was completely flipping out from the impending embarrassment of being the first scalp after I'd made such a big deal of telling everyone back home that I was going to be gone for seven weeks. On top of that I'd packed the cutest jury wardrobe that, devastatingly, no-one was going to get to see. And I couldn't disappoint Tom. I just couldn't.

I had been hoping to spend the first few weeks flying under the radar, but my body had failed me, so I needed to work out how to save myself. Tribal council was looming and I had about three hours to perform a miracle. I had become friendly with a couple of the female athletes so my first experience of strategy was scrambling and working on them in a way that was a *Survivor* fan's dream, but honestly it's not as fun as it looks. Actually, it was awful. The prospect of being the first boot was so stressful that I felt physically sick and embarrassed at the thought of it. I did, however, enjoy the fact that we had all signed a contract that sanctioned lying and deception, something we would never get in real life, so I really tried to embrace it. Despite all of my Catholic guilt, it felt good.

My wicked ways worked because I managed to turn the tables on someone else with minutes to spare. It was a miracle. *God must be okay with all of this deception then,* I thought. *Maybe He is a* Survivor *fan?* I was beyond elated to have survived, even though the next day I hid in the bush alone begging the same God to let me get voted out because I was hating it. I was homesick and miserable, plus the challenges were actually terrifying to me. I wanted to go home. But then, just before every tribal council, I would fight to the death to stay. It sounds odd, but I don't think it is unusual.

The day after surviving that first vote, I was walking to the well with Janine and trying to bond with her so I said, 'Thanks for not voting for me last night.' She looked at me blankly and said, 'Oh, but I did!' We both burst out laughing, and I thought, *Did we just become best friends?* Turns out, we did.

Janine and I met up with two of the non-athlete boys at the well and began scheming with them about starting an alliance of four that we could then grow to six. Our new family was created and the six of us – Janine, Abbey, Luke, Dave, Ross and I – were a force to be reckoned with. We stayed a strong unit until we tribe swapped. Together we decimated the athletes' alliance and took control of our tribe. It was the stuff *Survivor* dreams are made of.

I loved our gang, and on top of that, Janine and Abbey became everything to me out there. We were a power woman trio. I love watching a strong female alliance and ours was a special one. Janine was the strategist, Abbey was the physical threat and I was the social player. Between us I feel like we had control of the game until the midway merge and it was really something to be proud of. The fact that we are all still true friends after playing a game of deception together is also an incredible achievement.

◆

After watching *Survivor* on TV for so many years, having the chance to see behind the scenes was eye-opening. We were treated a little like we were army recruits in training. It was amazing how quickly we fell into line, even though the militant treatment seemed over the top. Before long I had reached a prisoner-of-war level of compliance and I fell into the groove of challenges and tribal council so completely that I rarely questioned the extreme nature of it all.

There was no greater horror for me than hearing the producer yell before a challenge, 'Water shoes, guys!', meaning it was going to be a water-based challenge, which I hated, or seeing the Tower of Terror set up for another death drop. I knew this would mean that we would have to jump into the water from a great height. Hideous. How people enjoy jumping from high things into water is a mystery to me. Even though my pre-*Survivor* training had included jumping off diving boards, I hated facing that tower every single time. It never got easier, even though we jumped off that terrifying structure so many times. I've heard exposure therapy is helpful for some people, but it definitely was not for me. I am broken. Now I struggle to go on a Ferris wheel. I even chickened out of Splash Mountain at Disneyland. I know, I know, it's not even that high.

Trauma aside, I did learn a few things. One is that I did not miss my phone at all, not one bit, although I would have sold a kidney to watch a football game, a movie or, ironically, an episode of *Survivor*. Another was that I realised that to survive I should just surrender to the experience rather than trying to mentally control something that was out of my control. After jumping off the Tower of Terror, my fear of challenges became crippling. I would obsess over what was coming and beg God to get me voted out. (Common theme.) Then, just before tribal council, I would beg God to not let me get voted out. (Here I go again.) It made no sense and I'm pretty sure if there is a God, She or He wouldn't have been checking in with some chick playing *Survivor*. Probably more important things to do.

So, after making my billionth random deal with the universe, I told myself, 'Okay, well, the worst thing that can happen is that I can't do the challenge and I get sent home embarrassed.' I decided to surrender to what was going to happen and stop all of the mental gymnastics.

It worked. I have never forgotten it. When I started to obsess over random things, I would take a deep breath and repeat, 'Surrender.' It might sound a bit wanky, but it actually saved me. I broke my habit of years of trying to control the world around me with obsessive thinking and praying to the air by simply surrendering to the unknown. So even though I left *Survivor* broken in some ways, I was healed in others.

◆

Just over two weeks in, a tribe swap was upon us. To say I got lucky was an understatement. I moved over to the Contenders camp and found myself in the majority with my favourite boys, Ross and Simon, as well as my girl gang, Janine and Abbey. You need luck to win *Survivor*; there are absolutely other things at play out there, but without some random luck, I think it's almost impossible to win. This was my lucky break.

All we had to do was keep our alliance loyal and then it was an easy ride to merge. The girls and I became closer in our power trio and we plotted our path to the end. Janine and I were in each other's pocket at this point in the game, which felt great because I knew if I got to merge, we could be a dangerous duo. The pre-merge game was always going to be hard for me because of the group challenges (yes, Reddit, I know I sucked at them!), but the post-merge game was an individual one with solo challenges that suited me much more. My years of yoga were an advantage because the challenges were mostly the 'Let's see how long you can stand in one spot for without crying' kind. Much easier for a small yogi with no sporting ability than a wrestling match to the death.

I was really starting to enjoy myself at tribe swap. I had found my people, although the pain of missing my kids never waned. My longing for them manifested itself as a physical pain that I could feel in my chest and it hurt all day long. The elements were relentless and sleep was minimal, but we bundled up together at night and tried to get a few hours of rest as we battled the bugs and the cold.

The worst nights were when the rain came. It would start with a *drip drip drip* and then you knew you were in for days of torture. Days and nights of relentless rain with no relief from being wet, wrinkled and waterlogged from head to toe, with no end in sight. Ross was great at predicting weather from his years of big-wave surfing and he was our unofficial meteorologist. I would ask him incessantly, 'When is the rain stopping?' I'd hang on his every word, hoping for good news. Now whenever I hear rain I still snuggle into my bed, so grateful to have a roof over my head. Sometimes Janine and I will still text each other on a rainy night just to reminisce and talk about how thankful we are having a roof.

On the flip side, when it wasn't raining and the moon was full, huge crabs would crawl on us while we slept, which sounds terrifying, but crabs meant food. In the early days we would scream in horror, but soon enough we were hardened and would pick them up by the pincers and throw them in the pot for breakfast. Sorry, crabs.

Overall, though the nights were long, arduous and some-what action-packed with strategy or mischief. My hips would ache and I would wake up every hour or so from pain, but my snuggle buddy Janine would keep me warm. Even though I soon realised I probably should have picked a fleshier sleeping pal, but cuddling her at night became my new home.

Fifty days stranded on an island with minimal food and shelter is a very long time, and this is way longer than the US version (just flexing here.) We got so hungry that we honestly started to lose our minds. All we thought about was food, all we talked about was food, and all we planned was what we were going to eat when we left. We would play games like, 'You have $25 and you walk into Coles – what are you going to buy?' Rotisserie chicken was generally the top answer. Or there was a game Harry, Baden and I invented called Mega Bowl, where we would fill an imaginary bowl with layers and layers of complimentary food and fantasise about eating it. For example, layer one would be party pies, layer two sausage rolls, layer three hot dogs, layer four hot chips and so on. (For reference a sweet version would be Pop-Tarts then custard scrolls, donuts, brownies, ice cream and M&M's for a topping. Amazing.) I also single-handedly invented a game called 'How would you cook each tribemate?' Ross was slow-cooked, Janine was stir-fried, Harry was skewered, Simon was a bolognese. It seemed hilarious at the time, but watching it back, I'm not so sure. I do still stand by the proposition that a slow-cooked ragu is the only way Ross should be served, though.

Perspective is a funny thing. When you are out there, life becomes clear and the smallest things mean so much. Memories of home are intoxicating and the feelings of loneliness are overwhelming. I was lucky because I managed to find a little piece of home in Janine. I wasn't there to make friends. I had planned to turn on everyone in a dazzling mix of comedy and ruthlessness, which unfortunately never happened. Then Janine came along and my best-laid plans went awry. Our relationship was instant and easy and I again had one of those moments in life when I knew I had met someone special.

I cannot imagine what it would have been like out there without her. I had promised myself that I wouldn't get into a power couple situation, but we were literally addicted to talking to each other. Most mornings we would make a pact not to talk to each other too much to avoid having a target on our backs, but that usually fell apart about an hour into the day because it was just too much fun being together. It was definitely a flaw in my game, but it was worth it because we laughed non-stop. Janine was my moral compass. I knew that if we stayed true to each other, that was all that mattered, and it was. She was my rock and if I mentally crashed, she would sternly tell me to pick myself up, which I did. We never questioned each other's loyalty, which in a game of lying and cheating is something special. I adored everything about Janine and I never tired of her company out there. Not once. When we returned home, nothing changed. How we still have things to talk about is beyond me, but we always do. What a *Survivor* love story.

I made other lifelong friends too. Ross is one of the most fun people I have ever met. He's a big-wave surfer with a lust for life and an enviable stockpile of courage. He was in his element out there by the ocean and we would sit up all night by the fire causing mischief until dawn. Unfortunately, a rope broke in a challenge and Ross hurt his ankle badly. Really badly. He was pulled from the game. It was hard watching the aftermath because he could no longer surf and it almost destroyed him. He is okay now, but for a while I thought he wasn't going to be. I'm so happy to see him shining again because he has a lust for life that is rare in this world. I feel lucky to have met Ross because I never would have if it wasn't for *Survivor*.

Janine, Abbey and I made it to merge together and I'm so proud of us for sticking with our female warrior alliance to get there. Throughout the game I was so obsessed with surviving the next vote (Sandra Diaze–Twine always in my head), but I wasn't clear about my path to winning. It's hard to negotiate making big moves while being realistic about where you sit in your tribe. You can't walk around swinging your metaphorical dick and try to orchestrate incessant blindsides if it's the wrong time, because you will just get your torch snuffed. Then, at the merge reward challenge, I won a phone call home where I was able to speak to my husband and kids. It was the magic bullet I needed – it flicked a winner's switch in my brain. It reaffirmed to me that nothing was going to stop me winning this. Sure, I was on the Champions tribe, but I felt like I had the heart of a Contender. I so desperately wanted to take home the title and from this point on, I thought of nothing else.

◆

Around the halfway point in the game, a producer gently asked me what was wrong with my face and whether there was anything I needed. I wasn't sure what she was talking about because camp was a mirror-free zone. I have melasma, which causes dark patches to appear on the skin, and it gets worse in the sun, so I thought maybe it was that. But the producer seemed really concerned. I asked Janine what was going on with my skin and she said, 'Something is really wrong, you've lost your pigment.' *Shit! Really?* I asked the set doctor to take a look and she suggested maybe it was from the sun, but I could tell from her expression that something was definitely not right.

I felt a bit uneasy about looking horrible on TV. I had already been worried about my possible moustache situation, but without a mirror I couldn't understand what was going on with me. People can get 'island hot' on *Survivor* and I had fantasies of that being me. It wasn't. I mean, we all want to try and look nice on prime-time tele, right? I had previously asked some of my tribemates to check for bald spots on my head because I thought if I was ever going to get alopecia, this would be the time . . . but they didn't find anything. Phew. I just didn't realise that instead of my immune system attacking my hair, it had come for my pigment instead.

◆

Post-merge I was savouring every moment and I felt pretty happy-go-lucky around camp. I played hard to win and while mine wasn't an alpha game, in *Survivor* you have to be realistic about your social cachet and play to your strengths. If you try to be something you are not, it's curtains. I recognised my place and knew if I was patient, I would be rewarded with the pleasure of watching the big personalities eat each other. They did, and it was extremely satisfying.

I had some patchy moments near the end when I had no alliance and so I stayed mute to survive. Around day forty, my game fell apart a bit from mental and physical exhaustion, but I pulled myself together in time for the home stretch. I tried to stay calm and keep my ego in check.

Ego and a power-hungry gameplay can kill you out there. It's what the viewers want, but most of the time it sends you to the jury. Inevitably, I went with my gut.

My end of game was better than I thought it would be, but it was also worse than I had hoped for. I was in a terrible position from final eight until final five. After that, Janine was booted and I was scrambling to stay alive and too scared to make a sound. I feel bad that I wasn't a better friend to Simon when people were mean to him, but I was dodging bullets so I stayed silent and left him hung out to dry. All I managed to say to him at camp was, 'Sorry I can't talk to you, they are all against me.' I still feel a bit shitty about it. My game instincts were right, though, because I kept the target off my back. That's the *Survivor* dilemma.

I don't know if it was the game, the yelling, the blindfolding, the fear, the scheming, the lying or all of it, but I definitely felt the darkness creep up on me in the final days. I also felt the mood at camp shift dramatically. At final four, I went into tribal council after a long and confusing day and sensed almost straight away that it was not going to be a great moment for me. It was the first time in weeks that I truly remembered I was on a reality TV show and it felt anything but good.

It's hard to go into it because I'm hesitant to talk about the machinations behind the scenes and I don't want to drag anyone down by defending myself. I can say that if you watched that episode, you probably either thought I was a cold, manipulative liar, or you thought I was a clever and intuitive player who respected the game by making tough decisions with heart. The truth is, as a player, I was probably a mix of both.

The morning of final three, we woke up early and as the sun rose a double rainbow appeared in the sky, which was beautiful and poetic. Those final days with Harry and Baden were the happiest I had out there. Final three can bond you for life if you get a good crew, and I really did. We were three peas in a pod for those last days, sitting up late and talking about video games and all the food we were going to eat when we got home. I was pasta obsessed, Harry discussed Pop-Tarts a lot and Baden educated me on the joys of bunny chow. It was amazing and it felt like a brilliant calm before the storm. Food and family were only days away and victory was coming for one of us, which was overwhelmingly exciting for three nerdy superfans. We had slayed all of the alphas and athletes who stood in our path and it felt good. I told Harry and Baden that I would write about us like Shakespearean heroes that rose from the ashes in a world that would never truly understand us. I probably didn't quite nail that melodramatic brief, but I hope I can make them proud.

◆

In the final days, I said to a producer 'Well, I bet you didn't predict this gang of misfits at final three!' She laughed and said, 'No I did not,' and even though she was being professionally upbeat, I was convinced that I could sense deep disappointment. She looked deflated, but hopefully she was just tired, like the rest of us. We knew we were a motley crew, but we didn't care because we had done something that not many people get to do.

The money meant a lot to us all, but winning the title of Sole Survivor was something else entirely. If it wasn't me who was going to win, then I was happy it was going to be one of the two boys. I loved those boys. They deserved to be there and I wouldn't change that final three for anything. My adopted *Survivor* sons.

On the last day we were finally reunited with our families and the happiness was actually hard to bear. Luke and I used to watch the family reunions and twenty years ago we made a pact that if I ever played we wouldn't cry, but of course we did. I couldn't believe I finally got to hug my babies. Seeing how much they'd grown in those two months made me overwhelmed with guilt. I'm sure I'm not alone in feeling that.

That day, we faced a hideous torture device challenge where we had to stand on pegs holding up sandbags for hours (six hours and forty minutes, to be precise). Gross. Luke stayed and watched me on the torture device and I could tell he was uncomfortable being filmed, but he did a great job of cheering me on and playing the part. Trying to outlast the boys was unbelievably painful, and I think it expedited a bunion on my right foot, but we all pushed through because this was our swan song. I focused on beating Harry because we had told each other we were taking Baden to the final and I was pretty sure I could convince Baden to take me. Harry annoyingly wanted to beat the record for longest challenge, which pushed us all to our limits. (Thanks, Harry.) When we finally made the record, Harry's legs gave way and he dropped shortly after. I followed suit pretty quickly. Baden took home the necklace and even though it sucked not to wear it, I was happy for him. I was even happier for me when he chose to take me to the final with him.

After the challenge, Luke had to go back to the hotel and wait for news of my fate. He woke up the message, 'Good news, Luke, she made it to final two!'

Final two feast and final tribal council – this is the stuff a *Survivor* superfan's dreams are made of. I made Baden a lovely plate of eggs and bacon and we had a champagne breakfast, which was a beautiful calm before the storm and a nice way to bond. I couldn't believe I'd made it to the final tribal council. The realisation that I was going to battle it out one-on-one was beyond my wildest dreams.

I've seen tribal councils get nasty, go too far, and I was scared of what people might say to me. Even though I felt like my jury management was solid – that's the subtle art of betraying people by voting them out while hoping they like you enough to vote you to win – juries can still be unpredictable. I felt sick about it all day, worrying that I might crash and burn under the pressure. I was so scared of winding up with egg on my face. I wished I had smuggled in a beta-blocker. Bugger it.

Once the final tribal council was underway, I started off a bit weak with my initial pitch as I was trying to be sweet and cheery. I looked over at Abbey, worried because we had turned on each other in the final week of the game so I wasn't sure how she felt about me. Then she mouthed, 'What are you doing? You need to fight!' She was still on my side and I was so grateful. (Thanks, Abbey.) She was right, too, so I went for the jugular. I enjoyed it more than I thought I would. I knew my pitch would be my weak spot and that it would the Q and A where I shone, and I was right. Baden nailed his pitch and I crashed, but he stumbled at the Q and A and that's where I put up an epic fight and was victorious. 9–0.

So I won. I won *Survivor*. I achieved an almost lifelong dream. I got every vote. I was blown away. I thought I was dreaming. I honestly felt like I was having a mental break, it was like that episode of *Buffy* when you realise she has been in a mental facility the whole time. I felt out of body and I wasn't sure it was all real. I was going to do so many nice things for my family . . . I could take the kids to Disneyland!

I've never been happier. I wish I could go back to that night, it was the biggest high I have ever felt. I don't think I will ever get a high like that again. I didn't think I could love *Survivor* more, but it became everything to me in that moment. Bigger than an AFI award, bigger than anything. It was amazing.

Then I ate.

I ate and I ate and then I had a shower! (The bloody outdoor shower in the hotel was cold, but I still loved it.) I shaved my legs, waxed my moustache (finally!), stared at my patchy skin and tried not to stress about it because I was so elated. I ate pasta, chicken schnitzel, chips, chocolate, ice cream, fries, lollies and two glasses of wine. I was basically the very hungry caterpillar with half a million dollars.

I sat on the couch for hours and told Luke everything that had happened, from the first day until the end. He looked a bit shell-shocked because he could tell I had changed; I came out manic, I was talking too fast and I was completely bug-eyed.

I rambled on at a million miles an hour about the first vote and Janine and Ross and eating termites and having to jump off high things and diarrhoea in the bush after food rewards, blindsides and relationship breakdowns. All of it. I told him how near the end I'd suffered through an odd and brutal tribal council and said, 'It feels like something bad might happen to me.'

He laughed and reassured me, 'Babe, it's *Survivor*, that's the point of the game. People love that stuff. As if anyone will care.' He knew *Survivor* like the back of his hand, so I laughed with him and agreed, but I couldn't shake the feeling. Then I went off to bed freshly showered with the happiest heart and snuggled into my beautiful babies. I held them all night long and dreamt of pizza.

CHAPTER TWENTY-THREE

Beauty is bought by the judgement of the eye.

WILLIAM SHAKESPEARE

I couldn't think or talk about anything other than strategy for months after I got home. Maybe a year even. Possibly two. It's not unusual. Most players go through it and some never stop obsessing. I didn't know it was going to be a long journey back to normal thinking, but for the moment I was just enjoying the freedom and the company of my family (although I already missed Janine.)

After I left the island I was grappling with a mix of excitement, bewilderment and fear, but the overwhelming feeling I had was excitement. It was a childlike kind of happiness I wish I could rediscover. Sometimes I think the motivation for players to go back on *Survivor* multiple times is so they can experience the unmatched high that follows you around for weeks after you leave the game. You have such a clear perspective on love and life, everything shifts into focus and it is pure exhilaration. Sure, for me it was followed by an epic crash, but I didn't know that yet, I was just buzzing with joy. My body was buzzing too. I could feel my immune system was overwhelmed and vibrating. I was twitching a lot, but that wasn't unusual and I thought a few days of rest would bring me back to normal. I couldn't get enough sleep, though – I slept and slept for weeks.

The day after my final tribal I was scheduled to go home, but our plane was cancelled and we were stuck in Nadi for a while. We were at a hotel with some of the players and crew which was nice, but I was struggling with winner's guilt when I was around them. I desperately needed space. I booked us a day at a nice hotel and we swam and I ordered a steak with bearnaise sauce and French fries and I had a long massage and paid for Lily to get her hair braided with those pretty little beads all through them. I guess it's how lottery winners feel and although I didn't physically have the money at that point, it brought a lightness to our mood and I felt a sense of possibility.

I stared at my skin a lot that last day in Fiji, wondering what the hell had happened to my face. I was so tanned and I had some patches of dark pigment, but the sides of my face were completely white. As I was plucking my eyebrows, I noticed that some of my eyebrows had turned white too, and I thought it was funny that I had never noticed it before.

Maybe it was the sun or maybe I had aged prematurely out there? I hoped it was a fungus from the dirt, so I pushed it to the back of my mind until I could see a doctor.

Lily seemed relaxed and although she had struggled while I was away, all that seemed to disappear when I returned. She had pushed through and now the epic reward was in sight – Disneyland. Jimmy, however, wouldn't let me go. He had reverted to saying, 'Mama' over and over while wrapping himself in my arms and smothering his face into my chest. Lucky for him, he was about to be partially cured by being locked inside with me for two years.

◆

I decided not to tell anyone that I had won, although someone from the set had leaked to my agents that I had made final two, so they knew I was a decent shot. I didn't tell Mum or Tom, but I did tell Nicole. That was it – I was keeping it a secret because I wanted to share the moment with them in real time.

The day after I returned from Fiji I was back at work on the third season of *Mustangs FC*. When I walked into the production office, I could tell that everyone was trying to hide their shock. I looked very different and it was obvious that I was skittish and completely overwhelmed. I had left a TV set where I was starved and blindfolded, and now people were offering me cups of tea and welcoming me with hugs and chocolate. It was a lot. The bright lights, noise and even the snack station were too much for me. I just stood and stared at the array of cookies in front of me, unable to make a choice because it felt forbidden while obsessing over how many I thought I could eat without getting caught.

I could tell Lizzie, my makeup artist, was shocked by my appearance, but my God she did a good job of pretending she wasn't. They all did. Those makeup ladies were such a support in those early days. I was finding the white patches impossible to cover, and the idea of shooting was confronting. It's such a strange feeling when you look in the mirror and don't recognise your own reflection, and as much as I tried to remind myself that it didn't matter, it's hard to break years of conditioning where appearance and self-esteem are intertwined. Lizzie calmly talked me through it and after she completed my makeup, I looked like my old self for the first time since I got back. Days later, when I walked in with a large new white patch in the middle of my forehead, Lizzie calmed me down and told me everything was going to be okay. That patch came up overnight, which was so upsetting because I couldn't make sense of what was happening in my body. It felt like I was being attacked from the inside. Lizzie and the director of photography would reassure me that I looked great before every scene, because they knew I was feeling vulnerable and scared. It was so supportive and worlds away from my

Survivor days, which were already feeling like some sort of bizarre dream.

While I wasn't feeling physically great, working on *Mustangs* was a lucky break because it was a show about female empowerment and I felt love and support from everyone. It was spearheaded by kind producers who cared about the cast and crew, and were passionate about the good they were putting into the world. Shooting *Mustangs* gave me purpose. I felt a sense of belonging. When I walked in one morning with an epic pair of new Nike kicks, the makeup ladies decided it was sign that I was Sole Survivor. It was. Rumours began on set that I had won.

A few days into filming, I was finally able to see a doctor about my skin. When it started getting worse in Fiji, the *Survivor* producers had been kind enough to arrange an appointment with a dermatologist, so I didn't have to wait too long when I returned home. I explained to him that I thought I had a fungus on my face from playing *Survivor*. He asked me what *Survivor* was and I proudly told him, but he seemed confused and unimpressed, which was mildly disappointing. He grabbed something that looked like a magnifying glass and placed it on my skin. When he put his eye to the hole to look, I heard him audibly gasp. That didn't sound good. That *really* didn't sound good. Then he looked again and his words were, 'I think you have vitiligo!', I felt a bit confused. I wasn't sure what that was, but I thought maybe it was that thing the model Winnie Harlow had. Before I could ask a question said, 'It's autoimmune, you have an autoimmune disease.' My heart dropped. I had a ringing in my ears and it felt like an atomic bomb had gone off in my brain. I knew what this was, I had seen my mum go through it and I knew what I was in for. I was on a bullet train where the destination was the complete destruction of my appearance.

The doctor asked me questions about my thyroid and my family history, but I couldn't think, I just wanted to run. He gave me a number for a vitiligo specialist and said not to worry because there were things they could do. 'If anyone can fix you, she will.' I didn't believe him. I had seen what happened to my mum. It was finally happening to me. Fuck.

I got into my car and cried and cried. I called Luke and I cried some more. I texted my mum and I could tell by her awkward response that she was stressed and triggered. I stared at my disappearing face in the rear-vision mirror and cried again. I booked the specialist, I booked acupuncture, I booked a naturopath. I thought, 'I have to fix this,' even though in my heart I knew this was now part of me and I never really would.

My career was over. That was my first thought. I'd never walk down the street again without people staring at me unless I had a full face of makeup. I wanted to die. I had spent much of my career wanting to be prettier, thinner, have bigger boobs, bigger lips, basically letting those bad messages seep into my brain rather than tossing them out. What a waste. Now my looks were being stripped away with each breath I took and it was the first time I truly appreciated what I'd had. I told myself that I'd never work again because actresses have to be perfect. I was flawed and disfigured and in an industry that values beauty above all else, there wouldn't be a place for me anymore.

I stared at my skin all day, every day, and I googled obsessively, but all I found was 'no cure', 'lifelong disease' and the dreaded information that I had a much higher chance of developing alopecia. 'Hereditary disease' was the thing that traumatised me the most because I looked at my children and realised that I had probably handed down my genetics to these innocent creatures. These sweet, beautiful souls who were growing up in the world of Instagram and beauty filters and the pressure of physical perfection penetrating their brains. How could I do this to them? I stared at my face and it was showing new patches of white every day. My eyebrows were slowly turning grey and I thought that my only option was to retire from acting and hide from the world. I couldn't handle all of these emotions, it wasn't just my life that I thought was ruined, but potentially the lives of my children. For the first time in my life I had an overwhelming feeling that I didn't want to go on.

I carried those dark thoughts every day for weeks before my appointment with the vitiligo expert I was referred to. Dr Michelle Rodrigues had a passion for helping people and the most reassuring bedside manner, and I finally felt a glimmer of hope. I didn't feel alone anymore. She sat with me while I cried and explained my fears and how I had seen my mother lose her hair in the most brutal way. I told her I felt like I was in a nightmare, and about the sense of dread I carried about passing it down to my children.

She listened and, most importantly, she understood and tried to slow down my mind. 'Let's just deal with one thing at a time,' she said. We came up with a treatment plan where I would use a cream combined with standing under UVB light for months to try to repigment my skin.

My husband dealt with it in a way that I guess I always knew he would, but it was still a lovely surprise. My skin had nothing to do with why he found me beautiful. Of course it didn't. He didn't even notice the patches, nor did he care. I knew that no matter where this took me, he would always see me as the most gorgeous woman in the room. None of this mattered to him, and that meant something. His attitude started to shift how I thought about it all. I began to realise that if I had that, then I had everything.

I went to my UV appointments and I tried not to stress. I stopped looking at women's skincare routines on

Instagram. My blood boiled when I saw someone mention 'flawless skin', or watched those filtered videos of twenty-year-olds rubbing oil into their faces cooing, 'Ooohhh, this product is how I have such a perfect glow!' Fuck that shit. No more.

◆

Eventually, it was time to watch myself on *Survivor*. Seeing myself lose my pigment (and my mind) wasn't as traumatic as I thought. I eventually put up an Instagram post letting everyone know what was happening to my skin and how my treatment was going, although I think initially I posted about it because I was insecure about how I looked. I didn't expect that all of this would change my life so dramatically.

The subsequent reception I received and the people I met afterwards didn't only change the way I saw myself, it changed the way I looked at the world. I guess my post was fairly positive, because I wanted to own it even if I didn't believe it yet, but I had the rumblings of something stirring in my brain and my sadness was beginning to turn to anger. My main message was, 'For anyone who has vitiligo or any other condition that makes you feel like you look less than perfect, I hope that watching me out there kicking butt on *Survivor* (and also getting my butt kicked) without a stitch of makeup on lifts your spirits. I'm thinking there are enough perfect looking people on TV, so I'm happy to offer an alternative and be someone who is perfectly fine with being imperfect.'

From that moment a tsunami of messages came flooding back to me from people who were all going through the same thing, some who had been through much more. Parents of kids with vitiligo or alopecia, people with skin disorders or disabilities who felt invisible because they rarely saw themselves reflected back on TV. People who just wanted a chat. I talked daily with remarkable people on Instagram. I immediately felt gratitude for the thing that I had been so scared of, and though I obviously still worried about the future, I felt like I had found a place where I belonged.

◆

When I started my career, I was fairly outspoken in interviews. I was a strong young woman fresh out of university, ready to take on the world. I had appeared in a great film that was a feminist and cultural think piece and I was confident in my voice. I felt like that person had disappeared with age. I wanted to remember how I sounded, so I dug up a couple of early interviews.

'There are roles out there for the girlfriend in the miniskirt but I couldn't put my heart and soul into something like that. I really hate watching films where the woman is the token beautiful character. So often you read scripts where there is a description of the man's personality and then the first thing they say about the woman is "beautiful, twenties". I don't want to look back on my life at eighty and think that I looked gorgeous and had the right clothes but maybe my whole purpose was to make other women feel insecure.'

I liked what I read. I remembered her. And I was sad I had let her go. I was so proud of these sorts of interviews, but back then I was told by my agent, 'You're too opinionated, tone it down.' (Don't worry, I have different agents now). Whenever I spoke up about this kind of thing, I was told no. No. No. No. So I listened and stopped.

Why did I fall into this trap? I think a lack of work made me overly concerned with how I was perceived and made me unsure of how to navigate everything. I wanted a good reputation, and the fastest way to get a bad one was to be a woman with a big mouth, so I smiled and kept my mouth shut. I was so worried about seeming 'difficult'. I regret that I looked in the mirror and questioned myself instead of questioning the world around me. I was complicit in believing that physical perfection is a glory to behold and if we don't possess it then we should stay hidden. What bullshit that is.

Things have changed a bit now. I feel like young women can be strong and opinionated and call out bullshit, yet Leonardo DiCaprio still gets to have a round belly and swan around with his girlfriends, who I guarantee aren't sharing his fries at dinner. We are still so used to this imbalance between the judgement of men and the judgement of women that we expect the perfect bikini aesthetic from the women surrounding these powerful men, but we don't require the same 'perfection' from them. He's Leo. He's a legend. He can have the fries. Actresses in Hollywood cannot, or if they do then it's talked about, they're photographed with the caption, 'She doesn't look like this anymore!' Sometimes they stop being cast. I thought ballet's attitude to body image was bad, but Hollywood is next-level.

Most Australian agents, casting people, producers and directors never really made me feel self-conscious and they certainly didn't ever comment negatively on my appearance. Unfortunately, though, Hollywood is held up as the pinnacle, so I think actors, like the rest of society, try to emulate what we see there and believe that is the gold standard. I know I did.

It took me a while to think it all through, but when the pigment disappeared from my face and my very first thought was, *My career is over*, I knew something was wrong. I eventually realised that I wasn't broken, the system was. Then something happened, one message helped me articulate the new way I saw the world.

Carly Findlay, an incredible person and passionate activist, sent me a message on Instagram that started with, 'As one of the genetically blessed . . .' In that moment, everything shifted. Oh my God, of course. I'd been led to believe I was not aesthetically lucky because I'd been trying to fit into a world that expected more of me than it should. I now know what it's like for people to stare at you because you look different, and I know what it's like to want to hide. I know what it feels like when children ask, 'What's wrong with your face?', and their embarrassed parents shush them. I know what it's like to hear people complain about their looks or ageing, and I can't believe I used to do that.

Carly Findlay talks about beauty privilege because a lot of us judge ourselves and our peers through this lens, but it is that lens that is broken. We hardly ever recognise our beauty privilege because we are given so many messages that lead us to look in the mirror and focus on what we'd like to change, not celebrate. Images of so-called physical perfection are all around us, in shopping malls, on our phones, on social media, in movies and on television . . . everywhere. Yet we forget that people with physical differences should feel beautiful too. The reason that they often don't is because the world rarely celebrates the diversity of beauty, and we can't appreciate physical differences if we aren't ever exposed to them.

Thankfully, things are starting to change in the wider world. It's slowly becoming more common to see diverse models in all sorts of contexts. We are all beautiful. Every child should grow up believing they can be a movie star if they want to be.

I regret every time I smiled sweetly and giggled when some American casting agent made boob gestures and suggested I should be sexier, or more womanly or bigger lipped or thinner. Every time I smiled and said, 'Thank you' as I walked out of a casting room, I left the door open for someone else to receive the same treatment. Rather than voice an objection, I swallowed my discomfort and allowed the bad behaviour to continue. I was wrong, but that door is now slammed shut. As scary as my vitiligo was at first, it isn't anymore because it helped me see the world clearly. I'm in remission for now, but I know if I have a flare-up again I will be okay because my mindset has changed. I have my voice back and I'm over in the restaurant with my 'imperfect' skin ordering extra fries, and I'm so cool with it.

CHAPTER TWENTY-FOUR

One's dignity may be assaulted, vandalized
and cruelly mocked, but it can never be
taken away unless it is surrendered.

MICHAEL J. FOX

'How will you feel about online bullying?' the *Survivor* psychologist doing my pre-show evaluation had asked me.

'Fine. I mean, have you seen *Survivor*?' I laughed. 'Some unbelievable stuff happens on that show. Those tribal councils have been vicious, people have cheated, stolen from each other, thrown machetes, hurled abuse . . . it's absolutely nuts. I know I won't do anything that bad. The worst thing I'm going to do is lie and play to win.'

And I was fine. For a while. I went to Janine's for a little party to watch the first episode on TV in real time. It was pretty exciting. I liked that first episode. I was kick-arse, running around saving myself. It didn't come across as brutal as it had felt at the time, and watching it gave me a smug feeling about how good I was at the game. *I was born to play it. I'm so glad that I will finally be known for more than one thing. No more 'We found Alibrandi' shouted at me on the street. If this is my swan song, it's a good one.*

For all of my mixed feelings about the *Survivor* aftermath, I will say this. Sometimes, when I am in nature or the air is crisp and the world is quiet, I miss it. I miss it deeply. There was something so magical about it, the people, the experience, all of it. Sometimes I shut my eyes and try to feel myself there again. It was both once in a lifetime and the time of my life. I loved those people like family, I loved that beach like home and the dirt was my safe space to rest on. I would lie awake and stare at the moon and think of deep things that passed me by in a world filled with phones and (ironically) reality TV. I get why people go back on the show, even though I never could. For me, nothing would ever come close to that first time – it was lightning in a bottle. I hold it so deep in my heart. I promised myself I would never forget all the things I learnt out there, but I'm afraid I might have forgotten some already.

I don't know how to talk about the rest of the experience without sounding ungrateful. I know there is nothing that annoys people more than a reality TV contestant complaining about an edit. I've heard so many times:

'You knew what you were getting yourself into', but I'm not sure I did, even though I probably should have. I think the problem is that I trusted who I was and I thought that would protect me. But that's not how reality TV works. While there are known variables in the game of *Survivor*, there are so many unknown variables in the game of television. Sometimes you come out on top and sometimes you come out on the bottom.

Near the end, I cast a vote with my final three boys and the viewers didn't like it. While the boys escaped outrage, I ended up being referred to in the media as 'the most hated woman in Australia'. Was it the edit or was it my vagina? Probably a mix of both. I was sent hundreds of vomit emojis and death threats. I got tagged in posts with memes of Liam Neeson saying, 'I will find you and kill you', and then a major publication shared that as 'news'. My kids' lives were threatened. I was seriously scared to walk down the street for weeks for fear of being beaten.

I played that game to win. A game that has been around for twenty years, with the aim to vote people out and lie to their face about it until you are the last one standing. So that's what I did. Pretty well, I thought. Then the audience wanted me dead. Wow, I was not prepared for that.

It's not all the audience's fault. In the storytelling, I took the fall. What reality TV does is it takes a thread of your personality and knits a jumper out of it, then forces you to wear that jumper in front of the world. Sometimes it looks good and sometimes it doesn't. It's not uncommon, so I should just put on my big girl pants and move on. I won half a million dollars. Cry me a river. But the thing was the lack of control I had over the situation – similar to my fear of flying. When you're watching your story plummet to the ground at record speed, it's awful knowing that you can't grab the wheel and save yourself. Maybe I should have been a pilot.

The more emotional the audience gets, the more social media traffic you get and, consequently, the more press you get. It's great for the show because people's comments on Instagram become news stories and then those stories get commented on again and it's a brilliant way to have a smash-hit moment in television. I get it. In the cutthroat world of ratings, it's clever.

Surprisingly, people in real life were lovely. I got high fives and lots of hugs from parents and kids, but on the internet . . . yikes. Thankfully, for as many people I had attacking me, I had people defending me too, which means a lot when you are suffocating in a pile of poo. These fans of the game spent their days and nights telling people on Twitter and Reddit to fuck off; I loved them. Their mix of insomnia and kindness warmed my heart and still does.

A year later, during the first Covid-19 lockdown in Melbourne, I watched *Survivor: Winners at War*, where past winners were battling it out for the title. What I noticed was the pain and trauma that some of these people carried around after winning. While sitting in one tribal council Sarah Lacina said, 'Just because a man and a woman are working together doesn't mean the man is calling all the shots. If a woman in this game lies or cheats or steals then she's fake and phony and a bitch, if a guy does it its good gameplay. What it is, is it's a gender bias, it holds me back, it holds other women back from playing the game how we should be allowed to play the game. I for two years have been so hard on myself from "Game Changers" that I felt like I was such a bad person. And I'm not.'

I immediately got a lump in my throat listening to those words because I knew exactly what she was talking about. Even a year after all that online hate, the pain was raw. I was really messed up for a while. When so many people tell you that you are a bad person, it starts to eat away at you. I was also mortified that I had exposed myself, and subsequently my family, and had lost out in the public arena. I was ashamed.

◆

I've struggled writing about all of this because I don't want to sound bitter. I hope it doesn't come across as 'Oh my

God, some people didn't like me, what a tragedy'. I just wanted to be honest about how online comments and some commentary has affected me.

While I was wrangling with how best to record my experiences in writing, I remembered reading a tweet a year after I played from the original US *Survivor* winner, Richard Hatch. It said, 'Gosh I wish *Survivor* participants who struggled with self-esteem or depression/anxiety issues resulting from their gameplay or media portrayal would have reached out to me. I have both the experience, academic credentials, and ability to coach folk through the process.' At the time I first read it, I felt a sense of relief that I wasn't alone and someone was on my side. I liked the tweet, took a screenshot and thought constantly about messaging Richard for the next three years.

For those who don't know or aren't into *Survivor*, Richard Hatch is a legend. He was the first of us. He is our father. He won the game with no point of reference, he didn't copy anyone or try to do anything other than win. He is credited with inventing alliances in the game because he believed that you couldn't win without a tight-knit group of people around you. He was right. *Survivor* is all about alliances and I didn't feel legit until I was in my first one. It all started with Richard, so I stan him very hard. His life hasn't been easy after *Survivor*, but he always stands strong, unafraid, unashamed; he is a true king of the game. He is worthy of his status as a legend.

So here I was, years after he posted his tweet and I finally had a reason to reach out. Tom was coincidentally staying at my house the night I sent Richard a message. I didn't expect him to message me back, but about ten minutes later he did. I ran downstairs jumping up and down. 'OMG!!! I've been WhatsApp messaging with Richard Hatch!!' We bounced around a bit and then I told Tom that I was going to have a video call with him. So we bounced around again.

You know how they say don't meet your heroes because they will disappoint you? Well, that wasn't the case with Richard; he was so much more than I could have expected. He was kind and gracious and, I realise in hindsight, he gave me a free ninety-minute counselling session. What a guy. During our video call, he said, 'I've tried to help so many. I can't tell you how many people are devastated, whose lives will never be the same because they are so distraught over what the public thinks about them. Are you okay?'

'Yeah,' I replied, 'I am. I wasn't always, but I am now. It took me two years to recover.' It felt good to say it.

He replied with, 'That's not bad, some people never recover.'

I told him that the pandemic probably didn't help, because I sat inside staring at the walls for two years post-*Survivor*, wondering if there would be more to my story. I felt ashamed, but also grateful for the money and the title. So grateful. Despite my mixed feelings, I still love the game of *Survivor* with all of my heart. So why was I caught up in the negative? It wasn't all bad. A lot of it was wonderful. Why did I ignore all the nice things people said to me? Why did the death threats and abuse ring in my ears daily? I guess I felt hard done by, so was it anger? Anger is hard to move on from. Or did I blame myself for not being savvier? Was I the problem, a bad person? Should I *not* have played to win? Do I have an unhealthy need to be liked?

I explained to Richard that now the world had opened up again and I could see my *Survivor* experience and the barrage of hate that came my way for what it was. It does, however, make me worry what other people on reality TV might go through. What about young people who haven't found themselves yet, or who don't have a supportive family – what's their experience? Richard said to me, 'These young kids are devastated because they haven't formed who they are enough. I was hoping that you had moved through it enough because it's about you getting to believe what you think about yourself.'

Thanks, Rich, I have. I deleted all the crap from my Instagram (it's my house so I'll keep it clean if I want to) and I never look at Facebook anyway.

As I write about this, I can feel a bit of that anxiety creeping back. I'm scared about people reading these pages and spreading hate online all over again. It's like that situation with the casting agent talking about my boobs – if I just shut up and play nice, then maybe I won't be the target of more online abuse and anger, but someone will be. Staying silent is not going to help them. Insults are thrown and lives are destroyed with just a few taps of the keyboard. This stuff hurts and kills, it really does. The media has a responsibility to not re-publish ugly comments or threats under the pretence that they're news or entertainment. They're neither. Re-publishing is just amplifying hate. In the past when I tried to open up this conversation on Twitter, I was hit with so much rage that I deleted my tweet and went quiet again. It's scary out there!

We have come so far regarding how we expect people to be treated in the real world, but it's the wild west online. It's the only place where the abuser defends their right to abuse and the onus is on a victim to just deal with it. I have heard more than once 'You're weak' or 'You should have thicker skin if you want to go on TV.' But why? Not everyone has thick skin and nor should they have to.

I know I'm not going to change anything with my mildly self-indulgent memoir, but maybe, just maybe, someone will read this and realise their words have power. Maybe they'll keep their opinions to themselves and change the channel if they don't like something rather than sending a death threat. People can hate someone on TV if they want to, but they shouldn't write to them about it. Just have a bitch to your friend over a glass of wine – we all do that!

At least the experience gave me the chance to meet my hero, Richard Hatch. We villains have to stick together.

CHAPTER TWENTY-FIVE

There's a difference between solitude and loneliness.

MAGGIE SMITH

I was on a girls' trip! I hadn't done something like that for years, maybe ever. I was in Noosa with some of my *Survivor* girlfriends. We were staying at Janine's house and filling our days with spa trips and late walks on the beach, champagne dinners and early-morning yoga. It was the best. I was still in *Survivor* recovery mode, but I was with people who really understood it. Smiling still didn't feel authentic and I wasn't as bouncy as I used to be, but I was getting there. Girlfriends help.

I remember it was mid-morning and I'd been lying in a big chair on the deck reading *A Little Life* by Hanya Yanagihara for the best part of two hours. The weather was warm but not too hot and the light was soft through the trees. I could smell the beach and I was thinking about taking a swim. I looked up and saw everyone on their computers, working. Abbey has an online clothing company, Lydia has an online sports recovery business and yoga line, Janine is a powerhouse businesswoman and Sharn is a barrister. I, on the other hand, like to read stories other people have written. There I was relaxing in the sun while my friends were making money and using their ambition constructively.

'There's some virus in China and I'm struggling to get my stock delivered,' Abbey said.

Lydia agreed, she was having trouble getting her merchandise shipped as well. They both seemed a bit stressed by it because they had deadlines. I was not; my deadline was finishing the book I was reading by the end of the holiday so I could move onto some Zadie Smith.

'I'm sure it's going to be fine,' I said. 'Remember bird flu and swine flu? It's probably like that, it'll blow over.' I started googling it on my phone, but it was so old my browser kept freezing, so I gave up. 'I really need a new phone,' I said.

A few days later, when I returned home, I popped into the Apple store.

'We don't have many iPhones,' the salesperson told me, 'there's some virus in China and we're struggling to get stock.'

'No way!' I said cheerily. 'My friends have small businesses,' I proudly told him, 'they were talking about the same issue.'

He shrugged his shoulders and gave me a weird look. 'I'd get this phone while you can,' he said.

◆

Things escalated quickly. Just weeks later we were stockpiling canned food and buying a treadmill 'just in case'. Then another week passed and the farewells began, because we were told lockdowns were about to begin. *Harry Potter and The Cursed Child* tickets were cancelled and refunded, and we stayed home and had pizza and watched the *Harry Potter* movies instead. My family came over on the eve before lockdown to celebrate Lily's birthday – a last hurrah. Not Mum, we were too worried about getting her sick. My nephews and sister were there, and we were all taking each other in because we knew it was goodbye. For how long? We didn't know. How bad was this virus? We didn't know. Were we all going to die? We didn't know. Did anyone have spare toilet paper? No.

We were all drinking the wine a little too quickly and putting on brave faces for the kids, but inside we were sad. I'd forgotten to the true value of my family until they were about to be taken away.

Luke's parents were in Queensland and all of a sudden that state turned into another country. We felt alone and isolated as we headed into lockdown. We didn't know that

Melbourne was going to close up longer and harder than anyone else. How could we?

Thank God I had put my winnings on the mortgage because we could hide away without the stress of needing to pay off the house. We were the lucky ones. Even though our place was tiny there was something about us all being on top of each other that I didn't hate. Waking up knowing the kids would be with me all day was comforting. We had nowhere to be, nothing to do except be together, and they were safe with me. Safe and close, it eased my anxiety about this bloody virus.

In Melbourne most of us got through the first lockdown okay. There was a long while when we were only allowed outside for an hour a day with masks on, so we walked the streets and rode our bikes, masked and compliant, because we were scared and confused. There was a malaise that stopped me from being motivated or enthused by life. I watched some good TV; *Better Things* and *Survivor: Winners at War* were my saviours. I thought I might learn to crochet like Nonna, but I didn't. Instead I made a five-star island on Animal Crossing. Gosh, I haven't been there for so long, I hope Tom Nook isn't too mad at me. I did make sourdough twice . . . First time was awesome, second time turned into a pile of shit, so I gave up. Lily and I watched every episode of *Buffy* together, which was bonding even if I was disappointed that Spike wasn't as hot as I remembered. My children started retreating to their rooms and their devices, desperate to connect with friends, and I didn't have the heart to step in and be screen-time cop too often. All normal; everyone went through it, but we all went through it alone, so it was hard.

We had a reprieve around Christmas of 2020, and being with family again was the best. We all rushed out to get our vaccine, we wanted to do the right thing for everyone and for our families, so I was happy to see my loved ones. I just wanted everything back to normal.

Luke had been up and down a lot to Queensland in between lockdowns to check on his parents, who we all missed very much. They were ailing and it was stressful for him knowing he couldn't just fly up and down whenever he wanted. A lot of people went through this and it wasn't easy. There was a divide between states and no-one was more shunned than Melbourne, so we had to jump at any opportunity to get there.

The minute we could, the whole family travelled up to visit them. Luke's mum had been put into care and his dad was alone at home, so I cleaned out the fridge and made him some lasagna and pasta to freeze, but I could tell things were going downhill. When we were there, there was news of another small outbreak starting in Melbourne.

We managed a trip to a theme park and one of the workers there said to me, 'Be careful. Apparently there are some Melbourne people here today,' and then screwed up her face in disgust. Thanks for letting me know!

On our last day in Queensland, we all turned up to the home where Luke's mum was in the activity room with loads of other residents listening to an older man with a cowboy hat play Slim Dusty on his guitar. The singer was buoyant, charming and full of life, and he sang with great enthusiasm. His wife, on the other hand, had lost the life in her eyes and could no longer walk and could barely speak. But when he played and sang, she would spark up, clapping and singing along loudly. I could glimpse the youthful love between them. She screamed, 'More!' whenever he stopped and he would smile and play one more. I could feel the cruelty of loving someone for a lifetime because we all reach the end in different ways.

My kids loved the show. James was sitting on his poppy's lap, clapping and listening, and Lily was sitting next to her beloved grandmother, Hanna, as she smiled, the first true smile I had seen from her in ages. It was magical and beautiful, but I could feel the weight of it all. The pandemic wasn't over and I sensed us gathering like this was a monumental moment, but I didn't know why. It was perfect, beautiful and poetic.

Luke's dad was one of the brightest souls I ever met, full of life, handy with his hands, a passionate gardener and the keeper of old-school ethics and charm. He was like a heritage-listed building in human form. When we left to go home, James held on to his poppy and sobbed, he never wanted to leave him. He worshipped him. But we needed to get home. The kids needed to get back to school because they'd missed so much, and Tuffy, my beloved silky, was old and sick, and we had to look after him before he died. We'd be back, of course we would.

Only a few days later, Luke rushed back to Queensland to be with his dad, who had deteriorated quickly. I held the fort in lockdown. Luke looked after his parents. Fast forward five weeks and his dad begged him to go home and rest. Luke needed a refresh and was desperate to see us, so he came home, thinking that lockdown should be over soon. He also needed to say goodbye to Tuffy.

◆

Lockdown was good for Tuffy. He loved those two years of us being home; he could barely see and didn't want to walk anymore so having us home for his last chapter was beautiful. Sixteen years is a good innings, I know. It wasn't enough for me, but it was time. We said goodbye to Tuffy, my first-born child. Love of my life. I cried for weeks. That's how it rolls with dogs because they are pure love with no complications. We need to work out a pill to keep them alive longer because it's been two years and I still miss my anxious little soulmate curled up at my feet.

By this stage you know I'm superstitious, something Nonna passed down to me. I throw salt over my shoulder when I spill it, I spit on myself when I get a compliment and I will never walk under a ladder. Fuck opening an umbrella inside. I've always had this fear that when a dog dies, it means a person will die – did I read that or make it up? I don't know, but when Tuffy died, I knew something was coming.

Lockdown dragged on and on and Luke's dad was getting sicker and sicker, but by then we were locked out of Queensland. We tried to apply for a permit to get over the border, but we were also scared of taking Covid to the aged-care facility where both his parents had moved. They wouldn't let Luke into Queensland so we anxiously waited for the vaccine numbers to rise so that he could see his father and hold his hand. Their long daily phone calls turned into short ones because his dad didn't have the stamina to talk. The stress was mounting.

Then, on Father's Day, while we were still waiting for the borders to re-open, Luke's dad died. He died alone. Soon after, Luke's mum died, as it often happens with elderly couples who have loved each other for a long time. Just two weeks later, the vaccine numbers hit the magic quota and the states started to open up. It was too late for us. Too late for many, I'm guessing. The news was filled with joyful reunions and crying families so happy to be in each other's arms. Unfortunately for us, we missed out on that one last hug.

Four weeks later the doorbell rang. A regular red-and-white post pack was left on the doorstep with no fanfare. It was Luke's dad's ashes. I guess they had lost him in the mail for a while. This incredible man was left for us on the doorstep with no more glory than some online impulse shopping. Soon after, we received another post pack, red and white. It was Luke's mum. That was the end of their story. That was the end of many people's story at that time.

◆

I'm not angry about the lockdowns or making judgements about what happened. I'm all for following rules. But I feel like we need to talk more about what it did to some of us. We are so lucky the worst is over and I am deeply grateful people were out there at the coalface trying to keep us safe. But it has impacted us all. Many of us have changed and I think to heal from the experience, we need to talk about the bad stuff a bit more. This isn't an anti-lockdown, anti-vaccine rant, it's just me pondering the aftermath of isolation, loss, death, separation and loneliness that happened in the process of keeping as many of us safe as possible. My parents-in-law deserved a better ending. They had a great life and knew they were loved, so maybe that's all that matters. But, as with Nonna, I never got a proper goodbye.

◆

This all got a bit dark. Sorry. Stick with me because I promise it lightens up.

Post-pandemic, I found myself thinking more and more about my nonna. Don't get me wrong, she's never far from my thoughts, but as I emerged from the gruelling separation and loss of the lockdowns, I found myself holding her memory especially close. And with world travel starting up again and the process of writing this book unfolding, I began reflecting on where everything for me really began: with Nonna, and her island home. I decided I couldn't write my story without going there.

When I told Dad over the phone that I'd decided to travel to Vulcano and Lipari, he was bursting with excitement. It's hard to get him to go places after lockdown, and his disability seems to be more of a mental barrier to doing things than it used to be, so when I next visited, we sat outside in the sun and got some air.

'Canetto,' he said, talking a million miles an hour, 'that's the little village where I'm from and it's in a place called Vulcano Piano. Go there!'

Since his stroke Dad loves to reflect on the past, and sometimes he chokes up more than he would like. He sat in the sunshine telling me tales of Vulcano – about the little house where he grew up, not far from his beloved godmother, and how most people in the area didn't go to school because they were too poor. He said Nonna and Nonno were illiterate, but life was mostly working on the land anyway.

This brought to my mind the funny stuff Nonna would do as she made her way around the world without the ability to read. I remembered her more than once serving me a glass of lemonade, which I would spit out because she'd accidentally bought soda water. Or the time she gave me an 'In sympathy' card for my tenth birthday because she liked the picture of the flowers on the front. When I opened it, it had 'Sorry for your loss' printed inside with 'Love, Nonna' scrawled underneath.

As I drove home that day, I thought about Nonna and her island the whole way, and felt sad that Dad would never get to return. I could tell in his heart that he would love to see the place one more time. There was terrible traffic on the drive home so I went a different way and before I knew it, I was driving down Grange Road in Glen Huntly. I spotted St Anthony's Church, where Nonna had died, sitting like a bright red beacon calling me to come in. I felt like all of this reminiscing about her and the islands had led me here, like her ghost was calling me. I needed to stop and see if I could go in.

The doors were open and there were a couple of people inside praying. I took a seat at one of the pews in the middle; it's where Nonna used to sit. I missed her, I missed being there with her and I missed the traditions she brought to my life. After a while of just quietly being there, I stood up and an older gentleman greeted me as I walked back up the aisle. I think he assumed I was wanting to find God, but it was close to lunchtime and I was really just wanting to find a sandwich.

'My nonna died here,' I told him. I was proud of her, it was a kick-arse gangster way for an old Sicilian woman to leave the world. 'In one of these seats she died, in the middle of church. She stopped the whole mass, there was a lot of commotion.'

He looked at me strangely, probably taken aback by my pride.

'I'm sorry,' he said. 'Are you all right?'

'I'm fine,' I said, and I meant it.

I was suddenly hit by the truth of what I was saying. I was absolutely fucking fine. My head was spinning. I finally felt like I was on the right track, that I knew who I was. And I knew I had to make this trip, for her and for me.

I walked into the bright afternoon ready to head back to the volcanoes that had been calling to me for so long. Ready to completely heal my heart.

EPILOGUE

Family is everything.

ITALIAN SAYING

God, getting to Italy is a trek. I have no idea how Nonna was able to manage on a boat for weeks on end while wrangling two young boys and dealing with the heartache of leaving her home. I was travelling back to her birthplace on a plane in economy class. Not such a hard slog in comparison, though I was missing my kids. At least I was able to binge some *The Real Housewives of New Jersey* in peace.

I'm so grateful that writing my story got me over there. I'd been worried about this book – getting sued, sounding whiny, having people hate it or hate me – but once I made it to Italy, I found I no longer cared.

The plan had been for me to head to Sicily, but it turned out Janine was in Italy at the same time, so how could I not spend two days eating pasta with her in Milan? She was a good sport, too, because she ate more anchovies with me than I think she was comfortable with.

Leaving Milan for Rome was a peaceful adventure. I've always loved train travel, but this was my first time travelling alone by train in Italy so it felt special. I was starving by the time I found my seat. That turned out to be a common theme for me on the trip: all I could think about was what I was going to eat next. Just as I was regretting my decision to skip breakfast, packets of green olives were brought around! Now that was adorable.

I was finding that people would keep asking me questions in Italian even after I said, 'Non parlo Italiano.' They'd keep speaking Italian anyway, only quicker, because I looked the part. And no matter what coffee I tried to order, I was always given an espresso. (I just went with it – I was too scared to order an oat latte in case I got kicked out of the country.)

When a mortadella panini was brought to my seat, it was just perfect. I was slowly becoming aware that I would likely eat my weight in mortadella before I left. It felt like the right thing to do.

◆

The train ride might have been amazing, but the next stage of the trip wasn't so much. It turns out I get very sick on a hydrofoil. I spent most of the boat ride with my head down, trying not to throw up, and those ferries go fast. I may have my roots on an island off Sicily, but it seemed I do not have the constitution to handle travelling there.

Just as I was about to spew into an old Chemist Warehouse bag, I looked up and saw Vulcano in the distance. I gasped so loudly that the man next to me frowned and mumbled some sort of insult in Italian. I'm pretty sure it was an insult because he paired it with a very dirty look. My inability to speak Italian became more of an issue the further south I went, so luckily I didn't understand him. But I wasn't going to let him ruin this moment. Then I started missing my sister, and I ruined it for myself anyway.

I wasn't stopping off at Vulcano just yet; the ferry was heading for Lipari. Even though my nonna and my father were born on Vulcano, Lipari was where they spent many years and where much of their family settled. Recalling the trip we had there as a family when I was young, I had wanted to go back. As we pulled into the port, the boat slowed and my nausea backed off. I could see the bright blue sky shining behind the rolling landscape of volcanoes that looked surprisingly familiar to me. I wasn't sure if I remembered them from my childhood visit or from the Isole Eolie tea towels that we always had at home. The port was filled with old fishing boats and the black sand peppered with volcanic rocks was beautiful. I may not have been there for more than forty years, but there was an essence of calm that washed over me as the ferry docked.

As I struggled off the boat with my huge orange suitcase and my Lululemon leggings, I felt like an awkward tourist. It seemed Italians didn't have the penchant for activewear that Australians have, so I felt myself sticking out a bit despite having all the features of a local.

Walking to my hotel, I looked up the hill at all the houses. It really was like an Italian postcard. I could almost see 'Greetings from Lipari' written in the sky. The sun was warm, but the air was crisp and lots of places looked shut up or were being renovated before the busy summer season. On that day Lipari was quiet, sleepy and filled with people I was probably related to but would most likely never meet.

I manoeuvred my way through the teenagers on scooters and pushy men trying to get me in their taxis and found the small, modest hotel that was one of the only places open at that time of year. An old woman was waiting for me on a couch in the foyer and she tried to talk to me in dialect. Even if I had been able to understand her, I wouldn't have been able to hear her over the TV blaring in the background. We both awkwardly laughed through our interaction, with her saying, 'No English,' and me saying, *'Parlo Italiano non bene,'* before she showed me to my room. There were brown tiles on the floor and a 1970s orange quilt on the bed that mid-century lovers would have admired. The pillows were flat and smelled a bit like old bread – I loved it! I sat down, staring out the window, and thought, *What next?*

Not surprisingly, I decided it was very important to find a *cunzato* to help inspire my writing. A blend between bruschetta and pizza, *pane cunzato* is traditionally known as a Sicilian 'poor man's meal', because it was created to use up stale bread. It's made with a thick slice of day-old bread, toasted and loaded with oily toppings. It was everywhere in Lipari so I sat down at the first place I spotted and ordered one topped with tuna, capers, mozzarella and tomatoes. Tomatoes in Lipari are next-level and the *cunzato* was perfect. I felt instantly vindicated for my love of canned tuna.

When I was finished, I went to the counter to pay and right there was a version of Nonna's swirly gingerbread, *spicchitedda*, that we used to make together. I hadn't seen the biscuits outside of our house before so I had to buy one to have with an espresso. When I took a bite I got a bit teary, but I was also quite pleased – it confirmed just how well I make them. I sent a photo of the *spicchitedda* to Nicole, and she immediately replied with a broken heart and the kawaii sad eyes emoji.

Afterwards, on a walk down to the beach, I began to feel guilty about my nanna and grandfather. I had so immersed myself in telling the story of my Sicilian family that I was scared I had ignored their side. They are a huge part of my identity too and a wonderful part of my life. Grandfather's family is from Cork, in Ireland, and I wondered if I should try to visit there as well to pay tribute. Possibly I was just trying to justify another epic holiday.

When I sat down on the black volcanic sand and looked out across the water, I felt a deep sadness wash over me. Life is so complicated and things hadn't worked out the way I thought they were going to. Not just for me, but for everyone. I was getting older, life was rushing by so quickly. I was missing my family back in Australia. And my dog. I sat there alone on the black sand feeling all sorts of emotions, and thinking about how one day, like Nonna, I would just be a memory too. Then I told myself to remember that life shouldn't be about mourning the past, but looking forward to what you've created. I knew I wanted to come back with Nicole and Luke and my kids, and share with them the sense of connection I had here.

I walked the island for hours that first day. I bought some Lipari t-shirts for the family and some Isole Eolie fridge magnets, then I kept walking. I was looking for something, but I didn't know what it was. Possibly an end to my book that didn't suck, but I wasn't ready to admit that to myself. Finally, I stumbled on an old cemetery. It looked like something out of *The Godfather*. The sun was setting and there were some women on a ladder fussing over someone's final resting place embedded in a wall.

They were purposeful and determined, stringing up lights that looked like candles and replacing dead flowers. I could have watched them for hours. I love the respect Sicilians have for death. They celebrate it as much as they celebrate life and there is a comfort in that for me.

I wandered away from the women and started to read the gravestones, looking for one of Dad's Lipari relatives. I was searching for the name Basile, which was Nonna's maiden name. I walked row after row. I started at the top and stopped at every grave. It was powerfully moving, standing there at markers of these finished lives resting. I thought of the people they might have been. Some loved, some forgotten. Just as I was about to give up, I spotted something. *Basile 1896–1969.* They were seventy-three when they died. I kept walking and reading headstones until I found another. *Basile 1903–1979.* They were seventy-six. Family. I sat down and quietly told them I was sorry I didn't know them and I hoped they'd had a great life in this beautiful place.

There was something about standing still in that cemetery. Like I could almost feel the heartbeat of all those who had passed before, and sense the way time meant everything and nothing all at once. The sadness from earlier was gone, but I started crying again, this time out of a strange peacefulness and connection to something much bigger than me (and also possibly from jet lag). Whatever it was, it affirmed that travelling to Sicily had been a good thing. I stood there until I started thinking of *spaghetti alle vongole* and knew it was time to leave. I'd find some cannoli, too. Nonna would have approved.

◆

I woke the next day feeling embarrassed about how I'd walked around Lipari crying and looking for gravestones the day before. I knew it was a bit over the top, but I was trying not to judge myself.

I started the new day stumbling through some Italian while ordering a couple of espressos and apricot-jam-filled biscotti at a cute little cafe. It was another beautifully sunny day and I'd promised my dad I would ride a bike to his old street, so I was catching the ferry to Vulcano. Luckily, I wasn't sick this time. (Note: if you ferry hop in Sicily, always sit upstairs on the boat.)

The smell of sulphur hit hard when I first stepped off the ferry, but after ten minutes it disappeared and the island felt like one of the most magical places on earth. Was it the light? The people? The active volcano? I think all of the above. Being there was exhilarating. The first thing I saw was a hand-painted sign on a boat shed that said in Italian, 'The monster doesn't scare us'. I looked up at the volcano, with its huge white cloud escaping from the middle and dispersing into the sky, and thought that it did kind of scare me, but it also kind of thrilled me.

I was determined to find a way up to the top of the volcano before finding Dad's street. Soon after, I stumbled upon a bike rental shop near the port run by a man called Santi. He talked excitedly about the history of the island as he walked me to his shed of e-bikes. I love how proud Italians can be about where they live; I just can't imagine giving someone a historic tour of Altona North.

When I told Santi my family's surnames, he lit up. He was so genuinely excited that my family was from Vulcano, it made me feel welcome and connected. I'd met a few Italians on my travels before who were from the island and they each had such a passionate love for the place. (Later on this trip, a man who ran a Catania hotel told me, in front of his wife, that she took second place behind the islands in his heart. You'd think that wouldn't go down well but she smiled sweetly because I guess she understood.)

Santi told me one of my relatives owned a restaurant which was shut for the winter, but he offered to call them and ask them to cook lunch for me. I was a bit embarrassed so I declined, even though I really wanted to meet them. He told me how I had relatives who ran boat tours and that both Lipari and Vulcano were full of people who shared my blood. He mentioned how so many of us had ended up in Australia after the war and he repeated the history that my nonna had told me about famine and struggle. But he also told me new stories about how, after the war, a virus killed all the grapes and when the locals couldn't sell wine, their livelihoods were gone. I wasn't as emotional as I had been the day before, so I managed to just take this in and not cry. It may not feel like a big deal, but hearing the stories of that place from Santi made me experience another eye-opening moment of time moving and standing still while whole lives are lived.

Once I was on the bike, I pushed hard, happily sweating from the first real exercise I'd done in weeks. I looked down at the sea and kept climbing, desperate to get to the top to see the beautiful view.

Santi had told me that all the locals lived in the Vulcano Piano, which is where my father was from. When I made it to the top I had to veer off a little way to find his street. People were waving to me and saying 'Buongiorno' and 'Salve' as I went by. The buildings had a festive Spanish feel, with prickly cactuses covering the landscape. It was gorgeous.

Eventually, I found the street Dad had told me about. The houses were old and there were goats in the front yards. It felt right. Goats are a big part of island life and I loved seeing them. Even the smell of them was pleasing to me. I closed my eyes for a minute and imagined the past. It wasn't hard to do as the architecture was so basic and everyone was still living a simple existence. For a moment, I had a wild fantasy about slowing down and retiring there.

Not far from Dad's street I came to a small cemetery, so of course I had to investigate. It was old but well cared for with fresh flowers on some of the graves. It didn't take me long to see Nonna's family name everywhere. So many Basiles were laid to rest on the island they were born on. We'd migrated overseas, but they hadn't. Was it better or worse for us? Who knows. I made a sign of the cross and said again, 'It's nice to meet you. I hope you had a good life.' No crying that day.

◆

I headed back down the hill at a pace that was probably a bit irresponsible for a fifty-year-old mum without a helmet, but I made it back alive and I couldn't wipe the grin off my face.

Santi wanted to hear all about it so I hung around the shed talking to him and his family. Before I knew it, I had a plate of rigatoni thrust in my face and I sat down on a plastic chair to eat it. It was covered in homemade sauce with tuna and whole cloves of garlic for flavour. The pasta was beautifully al dente; I made a mental note to take my pasta out two minutes earlier when I was back home in my own kitchen. I'd been really overcooking that shit.

Later, as the ferry made its way back to Lipari, Vulcano grew smaller and I thought of Nonna heading off across that same stretch of sea, waving goodbye to the home she loved. The island she told her mother she would never leave. '*Addio, ti amo,*' I whispered to myself.

Before I left Lipari I had one more important thing to do. Eat another bowl of pasta and have one more cannoli. Maybe a glass of wine. And, of course, some *spicchitedda*. Nonna would have wanted me to.

◆

I wish I could say I've learnt a lot about myself from writing this book, but perhaps it's more truthful to say I've learnt who I want to be and what I want to value looking forward.

My Italian heritage means a lot to me, but I wonder if some of that is wrapped up in how people perceive me. I look very Italian, I was in a movie about an Italian girl and I cook good Italian food, so the country is definitely part of my identity, but so is being Australian. I'm an Aussie with an Aussie family, and we love beer and barbecues and footy. (Go, Swannies!) I love my *spicchitedda*, but I'm also fond of a lemon slice. I am all of it and I embrace it all. I think that some of my tendency to look backward came from the love my grandparents showered on me, which was so deep I want to honour that and them. Maybe I also just miss the innocence of youth.

It's almost comical that I ended up writing a book about my Italian–Australian identity when I was in a film based on a book about the same themes. I guess that's why I made a good Josie, because inside us both is a shared experience. Many people who come from mixed backgrounds share our story and will know that a celebration of two worlds coming together is a thing of beauty.

Did I find anything profound in tracing back my Italian roots? Yes and no. I'm glad I went to Sicily, but the thing that overwhelmed me while I was there, and even now I'm back, is that it was hard to enjoy it without my family. My family is much bigger than Nonna Angelina would ever have imagined. We have become more. Different. My grandparents collectively come from Cork, Germany, Italy and Switzerland. Then I found someone who is Australian with a little more Irish added to the mix, and we had our own children who will grow up and hopefully mix it all up some more.

I still feel a little strange writing this book because I have a secret sort of shame about fame. I've been in the public eye longer than I haven't. That does my head in sometimes – if I think about it too much, I question its validity. Why am I worthy of attention and why would anyone care what I have to say? I occasionally wonder who I would have been without it. Nicer possibly? Less jaded? But then I realise I'm lucky to have had the chance to entertain and make other people happy. And what about all the free mortadella I've been given? That's priceless.

I always wanted to grow up to be like Audrey Hepburn – sweet, gentle and perfect – but as hard as I've tried, I haven't managed to come even close to pulling that off. I certainly can't please everyone. Can any of us? Probably not. And I really don't think we need to. So if @Aus_mum85 or @SurvivorJunki3 or any other critic thinks I suck, I don't care. Well, maybe a bit, but not as much as I used to.

After looking back at my life, I've recognised the one thing that really matters, and that's love. I hope no-one vomits into their Chemist Warehouse plastic bag when I say this, but I think it's what writing this book has taught me. I'm not a romantic and I get uncomfortable talking about my feelings, but love really is all there is. When I'm grumpy or tired or agitated by the fifty daily messages from school apps or sports teams or other stresses of modern life, I must remember that. I don't always have to look inward to find what's important because what matters surrounds me. That's all I know.

The other things I worked out travelling back to Italy and writing this book relate to the strength and courage of those who came before me. I learnt that bad things happen and we have to find a way to make peace with that. But, mostly, I learnt life is all one big messy journey and I'm not convinced that it's meant to make sense. We all disappear into the ether eventually. Then, before you know it, there is some middle-aged actress staring at your headstone and crying because you might share a drop of blood. Nonna used to say, 'Every day on top of the dirt is a good day' and I think she was right.

I realised, as I washed the smell of sulphur off my clothes before I jumped on the plane to go home, that while I loved it in Sicily, I couldn't wait to get back to my family in Melbourne. Back to where I belonged. Back to my beautiful life. And to where I can find cannoli and lemon slice, a good *napoli*, some Vegemite toast, a nice red wine, Milo and ice cream, biscotti, eggplant parmigiana, chicken Samboys, anchovy pizza, tiramisu and a tasty lamb roast.

PICTURE SECTION

From left to right

Page 1

Nonna Angelina and Nonno Salvatore on their wedding day

Nonna Angelina, Nonno Salvatore and a friend, all dressed up

Vincenzo at the family fruit shop

Miranda and Sons fruit shop in Glen Huntly, Victoria

Nanna Kath and Grandfather Harry on Middle Park Beach

Nanna all dressed up for a wedding

Page 2

My beautiful mum

Mum and Dad as bridesmaid and best man at a wedding in Glen Iris, 1967

Nanna and Grandfather with my sister, Nicole, and me

Me meeting a koala on the Gold Coast as a toddler

Nonna and me in the late 1970s

Nicole and me in very stylish matching velvet dresses that Mum made us

Page 3

Nonna and me on a ferry in Lipari

Nicole, Mum and me in Thredbo

Nicole, Mum and me in Lipari with family

Me looking quite angelic at the ballet studio in Melbourne

Nonna and me on the day of my First Communion in Darwin, early 1980s

Page 4

Rachel Rawlins and me dancing in the National Opera production of *The Pearl Fishers*, 1986

Me looking cute in a top hat at a ballet competition

Me in more fancy dress for a dance concert

Page 5

Grandfather and me sharing a Melbourne Bitter

Nicole and me in robes, getting ready on her wedding day

Me being stung by a bee on the set of *Looking for Alibrandi* (turns out I'm allergic)

Leanne Carlow (Sera) and I on the set of *Looking for Alibrandi*

Page 6

Kate Woods, Melina Marchetta and me in Taormina

Two shots of me in LA, 1992

Luke, Nicole and me in Singapore, 2001

Page 7

Luke and me at a photoshoot in the early 2000s

Luke and me on our wedding night, en route to nachos

Me posing for a magazine in the *Alibrandi* days

Me in *Vogue Australia*

Me in another magazine for *Alibrandi* press

Nicole and me hanging with Nanna and Grandfather at Christmas

My daughter, Lily, and me on her first birthday, 2011 (with a cake Tom made because mine looked terrible)

Page 8

Family visit on *Survivor*, day forty-nine

Johnathan LaPaglia and me after I won *Survivor*, 2019 (clearly, LaPaglias bring me good luck)

Me halfway up Vulcano, heading to Vulcano Piano where Dad was born

ACKNOWLEDGEMENTS

My Nonna's story was based on an essay I wrote about her when I was in high school. I was lucky enough to have sat with her when she told me about her life and I'm so glad that I got to document it. I was nervous about writing my own story and had so many false starts, but then I remembered the essay hidden away in a box in the garage and I knew I had my beginning.

Some of the names in the chapters on Nonna have been changed and I added details from my imagination, but all the drama was directly from her mouth. All the anecdotes were stories she had told me more than once. The feelings and emotions were the way she expressed them to me. And what an honour it is to have her story now printed in a book. I know she would have loved it. She loved a fuss!

Part of me hopes she is somewhere up there looking down and smiling, knowing that she may be gone from this world but that her courageous spirit will never be forgotten.

So, I would firstly like to thank Nonna for giving me the inspiration for the first chapter of this memoir, and for her boundless love and incredible food.

Thank you, too, to Nanna and Grandfather for being the best grandparents I could have wished for.

Thank you to my amazing sister, Nicole. To have a best friend as a sister is a lucky break in life. It's clear I have always looked up to you, so thank you for being the first person to read my story and giving me the confidence to put it out into the world.

Thank you, Mum – for everything. Too much to put on paper, but hopefully my love and appreciation for you shines through in this story.

Thank you to Dad for instilling in me a strong sense of self, for your upbeat way of looking at life and for the laughs.

And to my children Lily and James. You are my daily inspiration and I couldn't love you more.

Thank you to my husband, Luke. I hope this was a beautiful tribute to us. We did good.

Thank you to my incredible friend and manager, Henrie. My life changed when we met and without you this book would never have happened. Thank you for coming to Italy with me, and putting up with my indecisiveness about what restaurant I wanted to eat at. That day in Vulcano was one of the best days I have ever had and I am so glad we got to experience that together. You are an amazing person and a true friend.

To all of my incredible agents at United Management – you are more than agents; you are also great friends and are some of the most important people in my life. Tasha, Lee-Anne, Catherine, and Sarah – you have held my hand and been so important to me throughout the years and will always be. I treasure you so deeply. Trish, Laura and Wendy – I have always been so lucky to have you in my corner and I feel so appreciative for the years of support and friendship.

Shoutout to my nephews Harry and Cooper who I love so much and who I'm so proud of. I am the definitely world's luckiest zia.

To my parents in law, Aub and Robyn. We miss you every day.

A huge thank you to all my friends who I've mentioned in the book. You are in there because you have had a profound effect on my life and so this is a tribute you. I know I've left some of you out but there were too many stories to share. Thank you to all of you who are in my life, I am very lucky to have you.

Thank you to Melina Marchetta for giving me the gift of Josie and for your unwavering support and friendship. I am forever connected to you and that is a true blessing.

To Kate Woods for your passion, support and for giving me the best experience when I shot *Alibrandi*. How lucky I was to have you.

I have to acknowledge all of those who have given me the gift of working on a set or stage and to the incredible people I have shared those spaces with. Australian casting people are so encouraging and kind. To all of the directors, producers, actors and crew I have worked with, it has truly been an honour. Thank you for welcoming me into a world that I love so much. These are always the happiest times for me. I hope we get to tell more stories together.

I bow down to all of the *Survivor* players who came before me. I studied you and worshipped you and without you I would never have won the title. Forever grateful to my *Survivor* jury for voting for me – Simon, David, Sean, Daisy, Harry, Johnny, Luke, Janine and Abbey – and of course to Baden. And to all of the hardcore *Survivor* fans who sent me love, who came to my aid and called me Queen or Mother. Thank you.

To Carly Findlay. Thank you for all of your support. I am so appreciative of the notes you gave me on this book and will continue to strive to do better because of you. For that I am truly grateful.

Thank you to the vitiligo community for being a constant inspiration. The people I have met have changed my life for the better in so many ways. The Vitiligo Association of Australia is an amazing support and resource, and I also recommend the Australia Alopecia Areata Foundation for anyone looking for alopecia information or support groups. For those interested in the ways we can promote diversity and better understand our own ingrained assumptions about difference, Carly has pointed me to two fantastic organisations: Face Equality International, devoted to better representation of people with facial differences on our screens, and Changing Faces, which supports people with facial differences.

Thank you to publisher Vanessa Radnidge for taking a chance on me and helping me so much through this process. Your boundless encouragement is so appreciated and together I think we found a beautiful voice. Also to Meaghan Amor, Rebecca Allen and everyone at Hachette. This has been a wonderfully supportive and positive experience. Thank you.

Lastly, thank you to Tuffy and Gizmo. For me, a dog's love is the icing on the cake to my beautiful life.

hachette
AUSTRALIA

If you would like to find out more about Hachette Australia, our authors, upcoming events and new releases, you can visit our website or our social media channels:

hachette.com.au

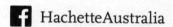 HachetteAustralia

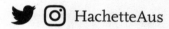 HachetteAus